Foundations

of

Fiction

Foundations

of

Fiction

How to write,
what to write,
and where to sell.

Christopher Carroll

McGuinn
& McGuire

PUBLISHING

Bradenton, Florida

Publisher's Cataloging-in-Publication Data

Carroll, Christopher Mark.
    Foundations of Fiction.
    Includes index.
    1. Fiction - Authorship. I. Title
PN3355.C37   1992   808'.025   92-80109
ISBN 1-881117-00-6

Library of Congress Catalog Card Number: 92-80109

Printed in the United States of America

Contents

Introduction

It should be stated from the outset that no one can teach you how to write fiction. So there is no misunderstanding, let me reiterate: No one can teach you how to write fiction. Writing fiction is something you must teach yourself. What you can learn from someone else is how the author uses the tools at his disposal to accomplish his work.

Writing is an art, it should be remembered, just as painting is an art. A painter is introduced to the brushes, the canvas, and the paint. He may be shown how to hold a brush. The actual process a painter goes through on his way to producing his masterpiece is a solitary one. No one can tell the painter how to paint a cloud. He must develop his skills on his own. He must teach himself how to paint. He does this through practice. The painter paints a cloud. Then, another. He keeps painting clouds until the representations of clouds on the canvas mirror clouds in the sky. The first attempt at painting, understandably, will not be entirely successful. The painter who keeps trying, though, will eventually succeed in teaching himself how to paint.

The same is true for the writer. As writers, we paint with words, and like the painter, we must perfect our craft on our own through practice. A writer may be taught the proper use of the tools of his profession, but, in the end, only through the diligent practice and application of those techniques, will the writer produce a literary masterpiece.

As you create your first novel, short story, or script, there will be no mentor looking over your shoulder, pointing out the weaknesses of your prose. In fact, the first person to judge your work, other than yourself, will most likely be an editor or producer. He won't know you personally and you may never see him. You will receive feedback. The first time out, this may come in the form of a rejection letter. Use that rejection to grow. Revise your work. As you get closer to something that is salable, the rejections may arrive in the form of a personalized note with constructive suggestions. Now you're really close to that first sale. Use the suggestions of the editor and give your manuscript one more polishing. You're on the road to becoming a successful fiction writer.

Accepting that writing is a solitary endeavor which can't be taught, the purpose of this book is to introduce prospective authors to the tools writers use to ply their trade. These tools consist of more than a typewriter or a pencil and a piece of paper. The fiction writer is a storyteller and his tools include everything at his disposal which can be used to build a story. Simply put, these include the characters in the story, the sequence of events that carry the characters through the story, and the message that the author, working through his characters, finally conveys to the reader. These are the basic elements of fiction, and their mastery will result in success for the writer.

You must realize that writing is hard work. If it weren't, everyone would be an author. Some authors report working fourteen to sixteen hours a day, some seven days a week. The average novel takes a writer anywhere from six months to five years to complete. That's not to say there is no room for part-time writers. Few first-time novelists have the luxury of leaving a steady job to devote all their time to writing. In fact, most successful writers today supported themselves in a miriad of other jobs while they learned their craft. What is important now is to realize that to become a successful writer will require dedication and persistence. If you have any doubts about your committment to becoming a writer, stop now. No matter how enthralling a lifestyle it may seem, someone who merely wants to dabble in writing will only find disappointment.

For those who take the challenge, the rewards are grand. The author of a best-seller could easily realize more than one million dollars in royalties. The rewards exist for publishers, as well. That is precisely why you have a chance of getting your first book published.

Using This Book

The contents of this book are divided into ten "lessons," each providing a different insight into the process of becoming a professional fiction writer.

The first lesson gives the writer-in-training some useful guidelines to follow to get started writing immediately. The second lesson provides an overview of the different fictional genre. The next six lessons deal with the mechanical details of writing fiction. Lesson nine teaches the essential elements of business which the writer must know. The final lesson pinpoints how to locate potential markets for what has been written.

You will notice there aren't a multitude of quotations from famous works of fiction to model your writing after, or from famous writers giving tips on how best to become a writer. Style in writing is individual. You will develop your own style. You won't develop as a writer any faster by trying to copy the style of another writer. In fact, copying may stall your progress. Because you will learn the writing process on your own, there is nothing to be gained from knowing how established writers write. Most famous writers are poor teachers. They don't know how they write, they just do it.

The hardest part of becoming an author is rolling that first sheet of paper into the typewriter and applying the first word. If you truly have the ambition and the desire to write, take the information offered in this book and start writing.

1

Twelve Precepts of Fiction Writing

You may be saying to yourself that a creative activity like writing should be beyond the limitations set by rules. At times, this may be so. In the beginning, however, until you are a published author, you must accept direction and learn the discipline of the professional.

This section deals more with attitudes and general guidelines, rather than specific dictums. They are, however, quite important to you every day. If necessary, write these twelve precepts on a piece of paper and keep it close to your writing area so you can refer to them frequently. You will find these precepts repeated throughout this text and will learn how they apply to the business of writing.

1. You must want to write.

This is the most important prerequisite to becoming a successful writer.

There are two main reasons why someone chooses a career in writing: vocation and avocation. First, some choose to write because of the financial rewards or the personal acclaim that comes from writing successfully. These are the writers who face their job as a vocation. Writing, to them, is a task performed for compensation. This is a perfectly acceptable reason for writing.

The second reason for writing is because a voice in your head tells you that you have something which must be said. You have a book inside your head that is straining to get out. You write because you must. Writing for you is an avocation, a passion. This, too, is an admissible reason to write. If you write because you must, beware that you don't lose sight of your ultimate goal: to be published. There is a tendency by some authors to become lost in the words, lost in the story, and forget about the actual job they are doing. If a story does not get published, it can't be read, and there is no use for it.

Whatever the reason for writing, it must be something you want to do. No one can force you to become a successful writer. In fact, a writer forced to write will undoubtedly fail.

Being pressed into service may not be in clear evidence. Any outside force which makes you feel you must become a writer will act against you. These outside forces may take the form of family members attempting to direct your career choice. You may be looking toward a writing career as a way of escaping an unpleasant work situation. You may even feel destined to follow in the footsteps of Hemingway. These are definitely the wrong reasons to write. Writing must be something you choose to do and you must be happy in having made that choice.

2. Writing is a business. Treat it accordingly.

Let there be no mistake, writing is big business for authors, publishers, distributors, artists, book retailers, and even the reading public. As a writer, you are the first level of manufacturing. You will produce a manuscript to which everyone between you and the public will add value in the form of editorial advice, printing, bindery, shipping, and stocking. You are the most important player in the business because none of the other activities can occur without your all-important manuscript.

You do have certain responsibilities which must be taken seriously. You cannot approach writing as a hobby. You owe it severe attention. Afterall, an entire industry is depending on your effort. You may have time to while away writing trivialities, but those who work in the industry don't. Consider that an editor, working for a publisher, may look at twenty manuscripts a day. You don't have any right to waste his valuable time.

If a book of inferior quality does get published (just look around and you'll see this happens frequently), the author is cheating his audience. The public pays millions of dollars annually to be educated and entertained by books. If they are deceived, the entire industry can be caste in a bad light and suffer.

For your greatest opportunity for success, approach writing from the standpoint of an employee and an employer. You are the employee working for the reader. Because your employer knows you are reliable and trustworthy, he allows you to work at home and set your own hours. You must, therefore, do just that. Set aside an area where you can work. It can be the dining room table, a corner of your bedroom, or anywhere you can perform the work of writing. Equip your area with the mechanical tools you'll need to do the job: paper, pencils, a typewriter or word processor, a dictionary and thesaurus, and whatever else you might need to carry on the business of writing.

Next, you must settle on the amount of time you'll work. This is the hardest part and where most would-be writers fail. They don't commit themselves to working at their craft every day. This is of prime importance. You must write every day. Each time you sit down to write you are perfecting your skill. Even best-selling authors who have produced a dozen books report successive books are better for their continued experience. This is truly on-the-job training. Set aside some time each day when you can work undisturbed: after the children are in bed or a couple of hours in the morning before you go to work. You could even rearrange your schedule to allow extra time for writing. Take your lunch to work and make wasted time valuable writing time. If you ride a bus or train to work, turn travel time into productive time. You may find you can get by with an hour or two less sleep just because of the intellectual exhilaration you will experience from writing. Writing is one of the few businesses where you can carry your entire office in a briefcase. Once you get into the habit of writing you'll find that your one hour will easily turn into several hours. It will be hard work at first, but you have to keep your goal in sight.

Writing is a difficult business in that the rewards you reap are often a year or two in the future. You don't have daily contact with a boss who might offer praise. You don't get a weekly paycheck that says you're doing a good job. Patience is the key. As you begin to write, keep in mind that the rewards will equal the effort. The more you write today, the sooner you'll get paid.

3. Read what others write.

Some schools of writing teach that you should read and imitate what famous classical authors have written. This would be fine if you were writing a classical novel. Today, imitation won't guarantee success. You have to find your own style, your own way of telling a story. You can profit from what others write; from your own analysis. As a prospective author, you must read everything twice. First, read as the public reads, allowing yourself to be entertained. Next, read the story again, from the writer's point-of-view.

For instance, if your goal is to write a romance novel, you should become familiar with the genre. From reading a number of romance novels, you can get a feeling of how another author tells this type of story. You'll experience how the competition treats characters. Do they appear real? You should examine what goes into a chapter. Consider how the point-of-view changes throughout the novel, or how it stays the same. Does the point-of-view change with the beginning of every chapter, or is the same character telling the entire story? Examine the description of locations. Read the dialogue aloud and hear if it sounds genuine. Take notes on your second reading. You may even want to outline the major events which constitute the plot: the conflict, the rising action, the climax.

The same is true for all the forms of fiction. You should not attempt to write a movie script without first reading a movie script. Samples of these can be found in larger libraries. Television scripts are slightly different from movie scripts and need special attention. Short stories, mystery novels, true confession magazine stories, and science fiction all have their own distinctive styles which make them different. By reading samples of the particular type of writing you are interested in pursuing, you will gain an important understanding of the requirements for publication.

A word of caution: Don't get so wrapped up in reading the work of others that you neglect your own writing. You don't need to read every novel ever written to learn the form that is followed. Two or three should be enough for a valid comparison. Remember, your time is the most precious commodity you have and you must guard against having it wasted.

4. Keep a daily journal.

Without doubt, some day you will sit down at your desk, clean white sheet of paper ahead of you, and stare. You will totally lack inspiration. The longer you stare, the more empty the paper will become. After a time, you will realize the two alternatives which face you. You can either put off writing until the Muse returns, or you can write on another project.

A daily journal will help you on either account.

A journal is a tool which writers use to explore. It is a notebook in which you record thoughts and observations. Whereas a diary is a personal account of the author, a journal should have a wide variety of subject matter. Entries are usually informal, but may take the form of a short story. It is your forum to write whatever thoughts present themselves to you.

For example, if you witness a newsworthy event, write about it. Describe what happened, the people who were involved, what emotions were present, what the setting was. If you have trouble getting started, remember what a newspaper reporter would ask: Who, what, where, why, and how?

As a writer you must hone your skills of observation. Remember, this is a business, so you must seize every opportunity for self-improvement. While you are attending a movie, you may see a young couple and overhear them talking about marriage. When you return to your journal, record what you saw and heard. Then, using that as a springboard, finish the story. Make up what happened after you left the theater. Did they get married? Or did the young man take a job in Belgium and leave his lady fair? Exercise your imagination. Practice your story-telling skills. All this is fair game for your journal and subject matter is ever present.

You can also use your journal for controlled, productive emotional release. When you have a bad day with your children or boss, turn that tension into something positive. If you are depressed, write something that expresses your feelings. Write about death and how it makes you feel. Harness your angry feelings and write a letter to your journal, saying the things you would never say to your boss in person.

If you can't think of anything to write, write about your lack of inspiration.

Your journal, like a diary, contains your most personal and private writing and should be shared with no one. Spelling and punctuation don't count in journal entries, although here again is an opportunity to improve those skills, as well. What does count is that you are writing. In the beginning, it is important to write in your journal every day. You may have to force yourself at first. Set a goal of two handwritten pages. You'll find shortly that you have more to write than you can handle in the time you allot. In these cases, make notes or a brief description which you can "fill out" later.

In addition to providing you with much-needed writing practice, keeping a journal provides a wealth of research material. In a matter of months you will have accumulated a volume of writing which you can draw upon for your stories. You can look back at the thoughts you wrote concerning the young couple from the movie theater. Or, faced with a scene in your novel which requires two characters to be in conflict, you can call upon the notes you made when you personally felt conflict. By keeping a journal, you should be able to bridge almost any dry spell.

5. Know your audience.

Always keep in mind you are writing to be read. You are telling a story and you must know who you are talking to. Visualize your audience. Who is going to read your story? Men? Women? Children? Children view situations differently from adults. You would certainly not approach a children's story the same as you would a story aimed at adults. When you write for children, your vocabulary should be simple and your plot not as complex. You should rely more on action than on emotions. And your characters should be ones that a child could relate to, characters they may have experienced before. The pace of the story should be faster and the length shorter, as children have a short attention span.

Before the manuscript reaches your ultimate audience, there is another audience that must be addressed: the publisher. Learn about the publishing company before you submit your manuscript. Some publishing houses specialize in children's books, others in romance or science fiction. You will be wasting your time, and that of the publisher, if you submit a mystery novel to a company that only publishes how-to books. The same is true of magazines. Your submission must fit into their format. Early in your project, you should develop a list of potential buyers for your work. After you have an outline, you should write a letter to several publishers, including your outline, and inquiring as to whether they might be interested in seeing your manuscript when it is completed. This is called querying. You may find there is no market for the story you wish to write and this discovery is best made before you have invested heavily in the project.

6. Write from experience.

To the reader, a fictional character or a fictional situation must seem real. Your job as a writer is to convince the reader that your story could actually have taken place. Even fantasies and science fiction novels must appear to be real or the reader will not be pulled into your story.

The easiest way to write something that seems real is to write something that is real. The images that are clearest in your own mind are those which will take form most easily on paper. There is no substitute for personal experience in writing. Even library research can't provide the vivid imagery you'll receive from standing in an actual setting and seeing actual people. What you see for yourself will remain in your mind for much longer than something you have read.

If you are writing an adventure novel set in Switzerland, your reader will know from the way you describe your setting whether you have actually been to that country. It will show in the adjectives you use. Even sentence structure can betray you. When you have genuine enthusiasm for a subject, your sentences will show it, just as voice inflection when you speak. Your reader senses this and will treat your story like a lie if he doesn't believe you know as much about Switzerland as someone who has been there.

Some writers try to overcompensate for lack of experience by throwing in trivialities which only a native would know. These trivial details can be drawn from travel guides and encyclopedias and disrupt the flow of the story. In these cases, it is actually better to leave out local color details than to force them artificially into your story.

If the experience about which you are writing is outside your personal body of knowledge you will have to acquire greater knowledge. You can research distant locations by going to those places. By selling the story you are researching, that trip can be classified as a business trip. This is just one of the fringe benefits of being an author. Traveling may not be the only type of research in which you must engage. Mystery writers frequently have to become experts on any number of topics including types of guns, the chemistry of poisons, medical terminology, and the like. This type of research can start in a library, but you would be best served by seeking experts to talk with. Go to a gun shop, visit a college chemistry laboratory, or take a class in medical terminology. All these activities will help you add authenticity to your writing.

7. Don't tell, show.

Saying that a writer is a story teller is an oversimplification. In the beginning, stories were not written, but were passed on verbally from one person to another. By necessity, the details had to be kept to a minimum in order for the story to be remembered. The concentration was on theme. Characters were few and might be decribed only as angry, jolly, or sad. Plotting was simple, with most stories taking place in a house, a field, or a castle.

By virtue of your ability to write a story on paper, you can create more complex characters and settings. In so doing, you can also make your characters more effective in communicating your theme.

For instance, you might introduce a scoundrel of a businessman into your story. You could tell your readers this man is mean, but there are varying degrees of meanness, so simply telling them what you think may not be as effective as providing examples of how mean he really is. Show your readers this man is loathsome through his actions. Show how he kicks puppies. Show how he picks the wings off flies before mashing them with the eraser of his pencil. Show how he, with no hesitation, fires an employee (an employee with a sick mother, no less) for leaving his desk after putting in only a fourteen hour day. This is called character development.

After you show your reader how your character acts, you won't have to tell them he is a scoundrel. They will have seen it for themselves, they will believe what they have seen, and they will remember it. This is the most effective type of story telling.

8. Get to the point.

There is nothing more irritating to a reader than a writer who refuses to get to the point of his writing.

If you find yourself counting words before you've finished writing, you may be guilty of violating this precept. Any story should have a beginning, a middle, and an end. In terms of plot, this is conflict, rising action, and climax. However, some writers don't realize that the climax occurs at the end, or at least near the end, of the story. That's why it's called the climax. These writers insist on expounding on the reasons for the climax, sometimes going on for a length equal to half the book. Just like in a movie, when the action peaks, the reader is ready to close the book and go on to something else. Say what you have to say and quit. If a novel is destined to be 100,000 words, it will be. If it isn't, maybe it should have been a short story.

Stream-of-consciousness writing is a method for developing characters and is generally a type of writing that refuses to make a point quickly. It was used in the early 1900's and basically put the reader inside the character's head. Every thought found its way to the paper. Because the human mind wanders among assorted topics, this type of writing was confusing to readers of the time. Even the critics who praised this form must have been unclear on its meaning. If you find your thoughts wandering on paper, start editing.

9. Follow accepted grammar, spelling, and punctuation.

You should have mastered these basic skills before you left school. Editors expect it. They don't want to have to teach you what you should already know. Mechanical mistakes in a manuscript can be so distracting to an editor that he will refuse to read farther. In fact, nothing gives away a non-professional faster than style errors.

If you missed acquiring these skills in school, you can compensate for it the same way professional writers do. Buy a good dictionary and a good style manual. Keep these with you at all times while you are writing. Some writers check spelling and grammar as they go. Others prefer not to disrupt their train of thought, waiting until they rewrite to make style corrections. Either way, you must become your own editor. A good editorial rule is when in doubt, look it up.

10. Be your own harshest critic.

Don't fall in love with your words. You must, as hard as it will seem, learn to judge your work first, before others. And you must be honest with yourself. If you read what you have written and it sounds senseless, don't think it will sound any better when read by someone else. The best way to judge your own writing is to put it away for a week, then read it as if it had been written by someone else.

11. Rewrite, rewrite, rewrite.

Once you have completed a manuscript it will be like a fat cut of meat. You don't care about eating fat and grissle, so you cut it away.

Before you sits 150,000 words. Now the real work begins. You should be able to cut out thirty-thousand words without losing anything significant from the story. They naturally will be significant to you or else you wouldn't have written them. But as your own harshest critic and editor, consider whether the reader will miss them from the story. Anything you can take out will make the story move faster, the characters will be crisper, and the action will be tighter. Any scene, any dialogue, or any narrative that does not contribute to the story is extraneous and must be eliminated.

Now you say, "What about those six-hundred page novels?"

The answer is, they most probably started out as nine-hundred page novels.

12. Be patient and don't lose your vision.

As I said in the beginning of this chapter, writing fiction isn't a way to make a fast buck. It isn't an easy way to make a buck, at all. Before you have completed your first manuscript, you should be in contact with publishers. After you finish your manuscript you'll be lucky if you have yet found one to publish your work. This is a time when many writers convince themselves they don't have what it takes, put their book in a bottom desk drawer, and return to a less-than-satisfactory existence. Don't let this happen.

Even the best writer receives letters of rejection. This is an everyday occurrence for professionals. But a rejection shouldn't be treated as a personal failure. Your manuscript may be as good as any. Your writing may be as skillful as the best. Yet you may still be rejected for other reasons. The publisher may have already bought a book like yours. Or, the last book they bought on this subject didn't sell well. Just because your book doesn't get accepted the first time out, it doesn't mean you should give up writing. While you are passing your novel, short story, or script around to different publishers or producers, start a second writing project. Although your emotions may not be right for another novel right away, you can begin planning. Or you may want to try another genre. If you just completed a mystery novel, write a short romance for a magazine audience. The possibilities are endless. The important thing is that you not give up. Keep writing no matter what happens. The chances are, if you keep trying, eventually you will succeed.

Writing Exercises

Start a writing journal. Use a spiral or looseleaf notebook and set aside at least one hour each day for writing in your journal. Also, establish a place where you can write. This could be a desk, the dining room table, or a corner of your bedroom. You must be comfortable and insulated from disturbances. Set a writing routine (same place, same time) and follow it every day for one week.

2

Forms of Fiction

One of the attractions of fiction writing is the boundless variety of characters that can be developed and stories that can be told. Different locales abound. And there are at least as many different themes.

Another attraction is the variety of media available to the author for communicating his story. These media make up the forms of fiction and include short stories, novels, children's fiction, theatrical plays, teleplays, and screen plays. In this chapter we will explore these fictional writing areas, called genre, and learn what it takes to become a selling author in each.

SHORT STORIES

Writers of fiction do not begin their career by writing short stories only to graduate to novels. Indeed, short stories may have greater skill requirements than novels. At the very least, they require a different type of skill. Writers of short stories may not make good novelists. The reverse is also true. However, writers in both genre can benefit from learning the skills of the other.

A short story generally contains between 1,000 and 6,000 words and presents a single theme with a less complicated plot than might a novel. Some themes naturally lend themselves to this form of fiction. Themes you find in short stories include jealousy, greed, love, and hate. In fact, any theme which you would find in a novel could also be found in a short story. The difference is in the presentation. The short story writer does his job with the fewest possible words.

The very nature of a short story means the writer must come to the point quickly and skillfully. There is no room for wordiness. Descriptions have to be kept to a minimum. Characters must come alive in a few sentences rather than a few pages. And the plot must move directly from beginning to end. This is not to say you can neglect descriptions and character development. It means you must harness all the skill you have to make these things happen quickly. If you were to graph the plot of a novel, you would see the action rising slowly to the climax. For every two steps forward, there is one step to the side. It is a jagged line. The short story, however, is a straight line, aways moving forward, always headed for the climax. Herein lies the skill factor.

A poet, through careful selection, can create an entire image with but a single word. Poetic phrases burst forth with imagery and emotion. Similarly, the short story writer must make every word count. A slip of craftsmanship may be disguised by the length of a novel. By the time the reader reaches the end, he has forgotten those elements that didn't add to the novel's forward movement. Those blunders can lose themselves in between all the pages. But the reader of a short story will remember the beginning as clearly as the end, since they occur only minutes away from one another.

Although the market for short stories is considerably less than in days past, there are some advantages realized by short story writers.

Short stories take less time to write than a novel. This gives two benefits in one. Because of its length, you know the entire story before you begin writing. The job for the novelist is not always so clear, as the novel-length story sometimes takes unexpected turns. Also, when you sit down to write a short story, you most likely won't get up until the first draft is complete. You could easily conceive, write, and polish a short story in a few weeks. The more stories you write, the better your chances are for getting one of them published. Which brings us to the next benefit.

No one will tell you that getting any piece of writing published is easy, but, even with a dwindling short story market, there are buyers of short stories. Many consumer magazines publish short stories. There are also specialty magazines (science fiction, mystery, etc.) which are filled with short fiction. And don't forget about the smaller magazines. They may not pay top dollar (or anything at all), but they will publish stories from unknown authors. There are also many opportunities in foreign markets. Or you might try submitting a piece to an anthology, a compilation of short stories from different authors. The more you write, the better your chance of making a sale. At any one time, you should be polishing one story while three others are in the mail and another is in your head. Once you see two or three stories in print, even if you didn't make a fortune from their sale, you can include yourself in that elite group known as published authors.

NOVELS

Novels represent a large and diverse area of fiction writing. Because novels target a particular audience, this area of fiction has been further subdivided into adventure, historical, western, romance, mystery, horror, and science fiction. These are by no means the only directions a novel may take. Many variations are possible.

A novel is defined as a body of fiction, usually between 75,000 and 120,000 words, which deals with a theme of significance.

Writing a novel requires a serious commitment from the author, as the process can consume six months to a year or more. It's easy for a first-time writer to become bored with the characters and the plot. Most readers, afterall, only spend a couple of days with your characters, whereas you spend day and night with the characters of your creation for as long as it takes you to complete your book. If you do tire of your characters, it's a good possibility your audience will tire of them, also. Remember, nothing kills a potentially good story faster than the writer's lack, or loss, of enthusiasm. Before you start, make sure the subject is something you are interested in and the characters are genuine enough to live at least through the final chapter.

Adventure Novels

In adventure novels the emphasis is on a fast-paced plot with the character or characters meeting a physical challenge and emerging victorious. The characters are often familiar to us without much in-depth development. Spies, explorers, smugglers, or the librarian who gets thrust into an adventure are well known by most readers. This familiarity can work to the advantage of the writer, allowing you to spend more time on plot development.

Of prime importance is the setting of your story: where the action will take place. Often, adventure stories are set outside, with the challenge being one against nature. The passengers of a ship sailing around the southern tip of Africa in a fierce storm, an explorer lost in the jungle, or an archeologist trapped in a cave while searching for treasure all qualify as a test for an adventurer.

The plot is a recounting of what happens to the characters as they conquer their physical test. Keep in mind that you must make the reader believe the adventure could have happened in real life, so the challenge must be plausible.

The ultimate compliment for the adventure writer is to have his reader exhausted by the end of the story. This can be accomplished through pacing. When the action is happening fast, your reader doesn't have a chance to take a breath, as when your plot flowchart (discussed in Chapter 5) takes many turns. The second method for making your audience breathe hard is through the use of suspence. In this instance, your reader will hold his breath, waiting for what will happen next. Will the mountain climber fall? Will our hero be killed by head hunters? Will the heroine fall prey to quick sand? The tension of not knowing the next turn makes for an exciting adventure story.

Although character development isn't as extensive as in some of the other genre, your characters must grow as they pass their tests. The naive librarian learns that books don't hold all the answers. The archeologist gains a renewed appreciation for treasures of the present. Or the most cowardly passenger on the ship may save the life of another and turn into a modest hero. The change must be present by the end of the story, even if it is a temporary change or one that is merely renewed or augmented, as in the case of a serial adventurer.

Above all else, the successful adventure novel should be as much an adventure to write as it is to read.

Historical Novels

An historical novel is one which is based on or suggested by people or events of the past. It is not necessary that these characters or situations be famous, though this sometimes helps your reader to accept your story as being authentic.

In this genre, the author is the teacher, presenting historical facts with the story. As teacher, there is a certain responsibility that accompanies this type of writing. Historical facts are easily verifiable, so it is important that you not present incorrect information.

For this reason historical fiction begins with research. It has been said you should write from experience. Unfortunately, few of us have experienced much of what is considered to be history. The cure for this is spending time in the library. But don't limit yourself to the library. Visit the areas about which you write. You can learn history by visiting museums, touring the New England countryside or walking through an English castle. Read the biographies of people who lived during the time you are writing about. There are no limits to the sources for accurate historical data.

By themselves, historical facts and figures don't make for a very interesting story. The key is in the presentation of those facts. In the historical novel, the writer speaks through his characters. They are the ones who are actually teaching the history lesson through their actions, their surrounding, the food they eat and the clothes they wear, and even their personal belongings.

These characters must come alive for the reader. The reader must be able to empathize with the character's situation. The conflicts of yesterday are the same as today. There is political unrest. Men and women fall in love and are separated by war.   Generations rebel against one another. The more familiar the conflict, the more real your characters will seem.

Secondary characters are especially important in historical novels. Their very existence can help set the time in your story. A servant girl in Elizabethan England. A telegraph operator in 1800's America. Or a World War II soldier. Any of these might be characters which have little impact on the plot but have a big impact on the flavor.

Care must be taken when combining fiction with history. Some writers will fabricate opportunities to interject historical references. The most important thing to remember is that historical details should be used only when they advance the story. Don't think you can throw in a fact here and there and have good historical fiction. If your reader can separate the fact from the fiction, you haven't done your job as a story teller.

Western Novels

Comanche Indians. Pony Express riders. Rustlers. The cavalry. Tucson. Fargo. The Rio Grand. These are the characters and settings which western novels bring to life.

The western novel is perhaps the oldest form of native American fiction. It started as a genre when eastern journalists ventured west in search of newspaper stories to sell back home. They found Indians. They found cowboys. But it was nothing like what they expected. The Indians weren't blood-thirsty, scalping savages and the cowboys weren't all six-foot heros. More to the point, it was nothing their readers would be willing to pay the price of a newspaper to read about. So, western fiction was born.

During this time, the newspapermen found real people to write about, and then embellished their lives to make them extraordinary. So we hear about a gunfighter who killed over a hundred men, the sheriff who spent the better part of his life tracking down this outlaw, and the traveling judge who sent this murderer, along with twenty others, to the gallows. No doubt, some parts of these stories are true, but the rest is what sold newspapers and novels.

Today, the western is historical fiction set in a specific time with a specific type of character. Readers of this genre are quite devoted and won't settle for trite characters. Writers of western fiction for modern audiences have learned that, to keep the story interesting, sometimes the villains wear white hats and the heros wear black hats.

The theme for this type of novel usually revolves around conflicts created by change. This entire period in American history is interesting particularly because of the contrasts. People in the eastern United States viewed themselves as civilized, while those in the West were looked upon as lawless frontiersmen. Conflicts naturally occurred when one group tried to bring about a change which effected a second group. For instance, many stories deal with the conflicts that arose when vigilante justice was replaced by new law and order marshals.

Here again, research is important. Avid readers of this genre will most likely have more expertise in this field than you. But you can add to your body of knowledge by searching out newspapers from the period and visiting historic western locations.

It is easy to get lost in the pageant that was the West. Don't try for a spectacle in every chapter. Focus on the characters. Don't make them out to be more than they possibly could be. Real characters in real settings make for a real western success.

Romance Novels

Romance novels, sometimes referred to as dime store novels or pulp fiction, are the biggest selling fictional genre. A single publisher may release up to sixteen different books a month.

These novels are usually written by women, or by men using female pseudonyms, for women. The stories are almost always told from the woman's point-of-view (see Chapter 4 for using point-of-view) and fall into one of several subgenres: historical, mystery, American contemporary, or international contemporary.

The key to writing a successful romance novel is "passion". The writer must create the sensation of passion. The reader becomes intimately involved with the heroine, feeling the heroine's problems are her own, becoming infatuated with the hero, and despising the villain. To accomplish this, the writer needs to make the characters seem as real as possible and to choose problems with which the reader can identify. Empathy comes from making the reader picture herself in the heroine's position.

The romantic hero must be larger than life. He should have a dynamic personality, combining strength with gentleness, and exude confidence and natural authority.

Reducing the plot of a romantic novel to its most basic form: (1) woman meets man, (2) woman has conflict with man, and (3) woman resolves conflict and marries man. What carries the reader through the story and maintains her interest is the anticipation of passionate love scenes and a happy ending. In these books, the hero always arrives, so to speak, on a white stallion and sweeps the heroine off her feet. The plot should have a hint of fantasy, or dream fulfillment, but still must be plausible.

These novels are frequently set in exotic, or mood, locations. Care must be exercised, though, so you don't let the location over-shadow the relationship.   Afterall, the two most important requirements for a romantic encounter, the two without which there could be no story, are a man and a woman.

Not surprisingly, the theme of the romantic novel is, without doubt, that love really does conquer all.

Mystery Novels

Mystery novels are the most structured of the fictional genre. Whereas the romance is a story of emotion, the mystery is a story of reason. Readers of romance novels find character interactions more important than plot twists. Mystery readers want to be challenged by the intricacies of a complicated plot. A crime is committed and, through careful evaluation of the clues, your hero, as well as your reader, will discover the culprit and solve the mystery.

Murder is the crime most frequently dealt with in the mystery novel. Someone must be murdered, or it must appear as if someone has been murdered. Murder is the most heinous of crimes and is intriguing because it can be committed by anyone if the conflict is of enough importance. The crime isn't limited to crazed serial killers (these characters will be dealt with regarding horror novels). In fact, the least likely suspect, the most even-tempered, mild-mannered character, is frequently the perpetrator. Even clergymen are not beyond reproach.

The mystery novel puts the emphasis on action, rather than on character development, although you can't neglect your characters. You must draw on all your skill to introduce characters that don't need much developing. The main character is usually one with which all readers of mystery fiction will be familiar, and can be categorized as: (1) the amateur detective, like Sherlock Holmes, who is intelligent, often financially secure, and who has varied interests, (2) the puzzle solver, like Perry Mason, who is quiet, thoughtful, and who thrives on determining how the crime was committed, (3) the private eye, like Charlie Chan, and (4) the spy, the smooth hero who has a way with members of the opposite sex. Or, you can invent your own type of hero. An interesting twist is to team an amateur with a professional. Not only do you get two heros, you also increase the pace of the story with interpersonal tensions. Maybe, in reality, it was one of the partners who committed the murder. A main character in conflict always adds to the story. This could be a witness who no one believes.

Other than the sleuth, your other characters, or suspects, will tend to be similar: similar in age, of similar economic backgrounds, maybe even of the same gender. Without spending too much time, you can differentiate these characters by giving each of them a single trait quite different from the others. One may have a twitch, another a limp. One could have a scar on his face that moves when he talks. Still another may smoke foreign cigarettes, blowing smoke rings out of habit. The point is, every character must be an individual in the eyes of the reader or confusion will result. In writing about your characters, don't concentrate more on the murderer than on anyone else as this might give away the secret.

For a character to be considered a suspect in a murder mystery, there must be three essential elements. The character must have had a motive, a reason for killing. Jealousy, greed, fear, and embarrassment are all valid motives for killing. Insanity is never a motive. The suspect must also have a means of committing murder. He must own a gun or have access to poison. And, finally, the killer must have opportunity. Opportunities arise when the servants are away, leaving the house empty, exept for the victim and the murderer.

Because readers tend to suspect the seemingly virtuous character with no motive or opportunity, the writer can use this character to divert suspicion from the real culprit.

As stated before, it is the action that makes a mystery. Plot, subplots, false trails, and suspence all work together to hold your reader until the final page.

There are two common methods for plotting a mystery. One is to have your detective uncover the perpetrator in the beginning and spend the rest of the story convincing others. An alternative, which is the more common plot, is to have the detective uncover clues with the reader and not discover the killer until the very last scene. Whichever method you choose, keep in mind that all mysteries have at least two plots.

The mystery is built around the discovery of clues. Clues point to the suspect. There are clues which are obvious: the spent bullet casing, the andiron spotted with blood, or the bottle of tequila that smells of bitter almonds (a sign of cyanide). There are also clues that require more careful examination. For instance, clues of omission (the dog that didn't bark because he knew the murderer), or the murder weapon that can't be found (a small puddle of water, the only remains of an icicle used to stab the victim). Your detective can throw off your reader by concentrating on little clues and seemingly ignoring the big clues.

Red herrings are clues that lead the reader in the wrong direction. Readers expect to encounter them. Trying to decide which clues are real and which are not is part of the fun in the mystery novel. In fairness to your reader, though, all the clues available to the detective must also be made available to the reader, and the murderer must not be introduced on the last page of the story.

The key to writing successful mystery fiction is to construct your plot like a maze that your readers wind their way through, savoring every twist and turn.

Horror Novels

What frightens you?

Do you fear darkness? Being alone? Does not knowing what lurks behind a closed door make you feel uneasy? Or does the image of people whose faces you can't see scare you? Maybe you fear insects or pain.

To examine horror fiction is to uncover the most basic elements of human nature. The fears you might have are shared universally. Masters of the horror novel, like Stephen King, use their knowledge of basic human fears to create stories which are terrifying.

The three most important elements in horror novels are character, atmosphere, and suspence.

The horror novel was once synonymous with monster fiction, but because readers know monsters don't exist, today's horror stories deal with real people who, by psyciatric standards, are insane. Everyone has a dark side. Under the appropriate amount of stress, this dark side shows itself. This is what horror fiction explores.

One of the keys to intensifying the fear in this type of novel is to make the reader identify with the victim. The teenage girl desperately trying to get away from the machete-wielding madman or a child trying to escape the grip of a hand which reaches from under a bed are both situations in which most people can picture themselves. Even if these never happened to us, we have all had nightmares.

Where the story takes place sets the atmosphere. Here again, the most familiar places will elicit the most terror. As a writer, set your story where the reader, identifying with the main character, would ordinarily feel safe. Many horror stories are set in the victim's home.

Suspence intensifies fear. The long build-up stretches out the climax and makes it more powerful. You can create suspence by the way you use words, stringing them together, building one after another. Start with "stillness in the air." There's nothing freightening about still air. Then add "silence." Make it "dead silence." The word "dead" prepares your reader to be freightened. "A night as black as pitch." Fear of the dark is basic. When your character finally feels a cold wind from behind, like breath from a corpse, your reader will be ready for a good scare, looking behind him to make certain he's alone.

Making the reader feel uneasy is the trick to writing good horror fiction.

Science Fiction Novels

You'll never find as great a variety of characters as you will in science fiction stories. Aliens, cyborgs, computers that take on human qualities, and genetically engineered or mutated humans are the cowboys and Indians of sci fi.

Science fiction writing, like many other genre, started in magazines. "Astounding Science Fiction" was the leading pulp science fiction magazine in the 1930's. Aficionados then, as today, bought all they could read. Buck Rogers and Flash Gordon were looked upon as prophets.

The science fiction writer of today is a writer of history before it happens. You step beyond what is known and project into the future. The writer can't keep making the same discoveries, over and over, so new plots must be developed continually.

In addition to being an historian, the writer also must be cognizant of science and technology. Advances in these fields occur daily, presenting new twists for characters and plot. Research is required. Writers should comb government documents and scientific journals for ideas. Sixty years ago, lasers weren't even conceived, but as soon as the technology emerged, science fiction writers were putting them to use for everything from weapons to surgical instruments. Again, they predicted the future.

Future is the key word. The writer uses the future to comment on the present, putting today's conflicts in future terms. However, the sci fi novel isn't a forum for preaching about the ecological ills of our planet, though this may be difficult to resist. You must combine an important theme with believable characters and an exciting plot. No matter how vital your concept, it cannot be carried by plot, alone.

The setting for a science fiction novel is important. These stories are set either on a different planet or on the earth as it would appear in the future. Much time must be taken with descriptions, since that which is unfamiliar is often more difficult to comprehend. Instead of straight narration, tie your descriptions to action. Let the characters portray the differences in the future world through what they say and do.

If you are unfamiliar with the science fiction genre, read a couple of science fiction novels before you start writing. Then, begin your plotting by playing "what if?" For instance, what if a nuclear war destroyed all life on earth and the planet became settled by aliens? Or, what if a space mission to Mars got hurled off course by a meteorite and ended up on an earth-like planet inhabited by dinosaurs? Or what if a scientist invented a devise that implants a tiny computer into the brain of a human, only to find the computer malfunctioned? Another technique for developing a science fiction plot is to cast a time-traveler as your main character and propel him into the future.

Remember, with science fiction, the fiction of today often turns into the reality of tomorrow.

CHILDREN'S FICTION

"Once upon a time, there lived a beautiful princess in a magical kingdom ..."

So begins the form and the genre known as children's fiction.

Writers of children's stories are often not taken seriously as writers. The unsophisticated may approach the children's writer and inquire when he might start writing real books. Though stories for children are usually simply written, they are far from simple. A completely different thought process is required for writing children's literature.

To begin with, the writer must think like a child. You must rekindle the innocence of youth so you can communicate one-on-one with your audience. Get down on your hands and knees and look up at the world. Remember what it was like to ask, "Why?". Remember the child-like creativity that allowed you to see a house or a spaceship in a single rectangular block. Think back to when you took for granted that babies were delivered by a stork and the sandman put children to sleep with a wave of his hand. Only by accepting that children live in a different world from adults will you be successful in writing for them.

Children's fiction is broken into three major categories: up to 3rd grade, grades 4 through 6, and grades 7 through 9. Beyond 9th grade, these adolescents are looking for adult fiction.

The first category is often the most fun, as it combines words and pictures into what is commonly known as a picture book. Although these are short, uncomplicated books, they still must have setting, character, and theme, and a beginning, middle, and end. And, they must communicate the story in about forty pages or less. That translates into about ten to twelve typed manuscript pages.

Characters in these stories are ones with which children are already familiar: giants, talking animals, kings and queens, dragons, and, of course, children. Not much description is demanded, or for that matter, desired. To keep the attention of a child, the story must not get bogged down in lengthy descriptions. You are competing against action-packed television cartoons where the theme develops from plot rather than character.

The use of short, monosyllabic words will keep the pace fast and hold a child's interest, although you shouldn't be afraid to introduce new, more difficult words. In children's fiction, the writer is the teacher. Children have an amazing ability to learn and will accept new words with vigor. However, you must make sure you use the word in context and lead up to it to make the explanation clear. A new word or two per book is great; you've done your job as a teacher. But a new word on every page will frustrate the child and break up the story so as to make it hard to understand. The general rule is, no matter whether it's short or long, use the best word for what you are trying to communicate.

Picture books usually take one of three forms: folk tales, fantasy, or talking animal stories.

Folk tales are basically updated versions of the stories that have been around forever. Classics like Cinderella, Sleeping Beauty, and Jack and the Beanstalk have stood the test of time. Use these as a premise and modernize them. You can recognize a fantasy story by the preponderance of kings, wizards, and dragons. In these stories, the hero brings a treasure back to the kingdom or rescues the princess.

Talking animal stories teach a simple lesson through the actions of the animals. The tendancy is to use animals because they are cute, but the only justifiable reason for using animals is to advance the story or because the story could not be told otherwise.

"Once upon a time" doesn't always have to end "happily every after". Children today are more sophisticated than in the past. They demand justice and they don't want loose ends. Children expect that good deeds will be rewarded and evil deeds won't go unpunished. They find security in this balance and won't be satisfied by a story that leaves them wondering what happened to the characters.

Children's books are meant to be read aloud. The best writers actually construct their sentences to reflect the natural pause created when the reader takes a breath. Learn to recognize the natural rhythm which exists between breathing and speaking and incorporate this into your writing.

Although the primary audience for this type of book is children, keep in mind that few children buy their own books. Parents, grand-parents, and teachers buy most of the children's books sold, so your story must appeal to them, first.

Whereas picture books are generally read to a child, books written for the next age groups are read by them. Stories written for older children and young adults have the same basic characteristics of novels written for adults: character, setting, plot, and theme. Although these stories are as varied as mysteries, fantasies, adventures, and romances, they always have one element in common: the main charac-ters are children who are in conflict with eachother or with adults. Children are egoistic and like to see themselves portrayed in stories. As the writer, you should cast your story with characters slightly older than your intended audience, as children always imagine themselves older than they really are. They identify with older brothers and sisters, whom they emulate.

Stories for these older age groups can be categorized into realistic fiction and fantasy fiction. Realistic fiction is set in familiar locations such as school, summer camp, or in the neighborhood. The characters are regular people facing and resolving conflicts which every youngster experiences. Falling in love for the first time, parents involved in divorce, or children being bullied are all real life conflicts which can be dealt with effectively in realistic fiction. In this case, the writer acts as an advisor, helping children realize their's are not unique problems.

Fantasy fiction takes place in a land of make believe or in an ordinary setting where extraordinary events take place. This is where ghosts, monsters, wizards, and space travel are frequent topics. Realistic fiction teaches everyday lessons. Fantasy fiction teaches monumental lessons, those which establish values. The most popular theme is good against evil. It's important to make your characters clearly good or evil since you don't want to confuse your readers with shades of gray. It is also important in fantasy fiction to avoid the abstract. Stick to substantial concepts which children can understand and feel comfortable about.

Children's fiction reaches beyond story books and novels. There is a tremendous magazine market for juvenile fiction, one represented by more than one hundred publications. Religious magazines dominate this market and usually require that the story has a strong moralistic theme. It is best to research these magazines before submitting stories.

Finally, a word of caution: when writing for young adults, avoid the use of slang and any reference to fads. Slang expressions have a life expectancy of five years and will date your material to the extent that when the phrases are out of fashion, so is your story.

THEATRICAL PLAYS

The theatrical play, a literary artform that dates back more than 2,500 years, started in Greece as part of a religious ceremony to honor the god of wine and revelry, Bacchus. The Greek tragedies of Sophocles and Euripides followed close behind, setting the stage for modern theater.

Today, there are thousands of theater groups in the United States, from New York's Broadway, to community playhouses. Many of these perform only the better-known, well-established plays of famous authors. However, there is a substantial market for new plays and promising opportunities for talented new playwrights. Smaller theater groups, especially, are often eager to review previously unperformed material.

To write a stage play, the author must realize the elements which make a play different from a novel or a movie. First, and foremost, a play is written to be performed, not read. Members of the audience are not able to see the words or re-read a paragraph that isn't clear. Important information should be repeated three times or the audience may miss it, and, you must keep reminding the audience of the main conflict as the play progresses. This will help the audience, as well as the writer, keep focused on the goals of the characters. Also, information usually found in a narrative must be incorporated into the dialogue without giving your characters long, boring speeches.

Other limitations of the theatrical play not found in other genre are those of setting, action, and time. In a novel or movie, the setting can change with every chapter, or even within every chapter, or every scene. In a play, the playwright is limited in most cases to changing the setting only between acts. Shifting scenery more than this will break the momentum of your play. The limited setting dictates that the action, or plot, be kept simple. Seldom will you find subplots in a theatrical play. There just isn't enough time to develop them properly and, if there were, the audience would need a scorecard to keep track. Time on the stage is real time. For a full length play, the writer takes one and one-half hours out of the characters' lives to share with the audience. It is difficult for the audience to perceive a time shift on stage when they, themselves, have not experienced it. In other words, don't expect your audience to believe that five years have passed between the time the curtain closes and reopens.

Finally, there are no close-ups in theater. Your characters' actions and reactions must either be exaggerated in whole-body movements or must be eluded to through dialogue. Every action must be capable of being interpretted by every member of the audience or else you aren't communicating effectively.

The key to drama, in theater as well as in any form of fiction, is conflict.   Conflict arises when the main character is opposed in progress toward his goal or objective.   Conflict can be internal, the character wrestling with his conscience, or external, where the character is opposed by another character, a group of characters, nature, or fate.   You must show the character in conflict, you can't just have him talk about it.   The conflict you choose should be universal, one the audience has possibly experienced for themselves, and, since conflict and resolution would result in a pretty short play, you must create obstacles to prevent your character from immediately resolving his conflict.

Characters are the key to communication in a play.   Through the characters the playwright sets the time, place, atmosphere, tone, and conflict of the drama.   Characters in theater must be different from the characters in a book.   Your characters will be with the audience for only a short time, yet the audience must become intimately familiar with them.   To accomplish this, make your characters more simple than they would be in real life.   This way, there is less information about the character you have to communicate. Because theatergoers don't pay to see ordinary people portrayed on stage, you must make your simple characters appear bigger-than-life by making their problems monumental.   The conflicts need to be of a life-or-death magnatude. Personalities are flamboyant or dismal. Disappointment turns to heartbreak.

The structure of a play is determined by the need to change scenery on the stage and for actors to change costumes.   The major divisions of a theatrical play are acts.   Each act usually lasts between thirty and forty-five minutes.   The acts are often further divided into scenes.   A scene takes place at one location at one time. If you shift the action to another location at another time, you have changed scenes.

It is important to remember that every act has a beginning, middle, and end.   For an act of a play to satisfy the audience, you must introduce a conflict in the beginning (which is a part of the overall conflict), create rising tension in the middle, and resolve this sub-conflict by the end of the act, thereby moving your character closer to the resolution of the major conflict.   Each act has a mini-climax which will maintain the audience's interest until the beginning of the next act.

For your first attempt, try writing a one-act play. There are many advantages to this. A one-act play is one-third the length of a full-length play, there are fewer characters to deal with, and there only needs to be one setting. Even though it is shorter in length, the one-act play should have all the emotion of a longer play. This is excellent practice and will give you an idea of what goes into writing theatrical fiction.

Before you begin writing your first play, create a simple outline to guide you. Include in this a list of the characters in your play and how you will introduce them to the audience. Write down the central conflict and possible complications that will arise to prevent your character from resolving this conflict. Finally, determine how the conflict will be resolved and how the characters will arrive at this solution. The story you tell must be strong enough to carry the play. A fifteen-minute story that's stretched into a one-hour-and-thirty-minute play will provide little entertainment for the audience.

TELEPLAYS

Everyone watches television. Television is a medium that first found its way into our living rooms in the early 1930's. Statistics show that children growing up today spend more time in front of the television than they do in school. Adults watch television an average of four or more hours a day. As a medium, this is the essence of mass communication.

You may have watched television without realizing someone actually wrote what the actors are saying. Sometimes it's hard to believe anyone would be willing to take the credit for much of what appears on television. But nearly every word that comes into your living room via television air waves was conceived by a writer; a writer who was highly compensated for his trouble. Everything from the evening news and late-night talk shows to soap operas and mini series are written before they are broadcast. Which means there is always a demand for television writers.

Television presents some unique problems to the writer. There is almost never narration in television dramas. The author must communicate through the dialogue and the actions of his characters. Unlike a theatrical play, the author can make use of the camera to let the viewer see and interpret the facial expressions of the characters and, in the place of narration, to establish a scene.

Perhaps after watching a situation comedy, you have said to yourself, "I could write better than that." And the chances are, you could. Although writing a script for television is difficult in itself, the hardest part of writing for television is getting that script from your typewriter onto the screen. Ninety-five percent of all teleplays are written by professional writers. The Writer's Guild of America defines a professional writer as someone who: (1) has been employed for a total of 13 weeks as a motion picture and/or television writer, or a radio writer for dramatic programs, or (2) has received credit on the screen as a writer for a television or theatrical motion picture, or (3) has received credit for three original stories or one teleplay for a program one-half hour or more in length in the field of live television, or (4) has received credit for three radio scripts for dramatic radio programs one-half hour or more in length, or (5) has received credit for one professionally produced play on the legitimate stage, or one published novel.

If you don't qualify as a professional writer as defined above, you still have a chance (five percent chance, but a chance, none the less) of breaking into television writing. You will have to prove yourself by actually writing a script and submitting it to a producer. It is not necessary to seek a non-writing job in the television industry just to get your foot in the door. Although there are instances of writers working their way up from the mail room, these people had the skill required and only benefitted from getting closer to the people who make the decisions.

A story written to be performed on television is called a teleplay. They can usually be divided into drama or comedy, with each of those being further divided. An episodic series is one that contains one or more continuing characters and will air over a thirteen week period. A soap opera airs daily, while most prime-time series air once a week. A mini series is one where four to six episodes air in a short period of time. Made-for-television movies are better handled as a screen play.

Your best chance of breaking into television writing is by concentrating on writing an episode of a series.

Many of the programs you view on television are series. A series actually begins a year or two before you see the first episode. Every year, the networks give money to the major production companies (Filmways, Fox, Lorimar, MTM, MGM, Paramount, Spelling-Goldberg, Universal, Viacom, etc.) to develop pilots. A pilot is the first show of a series which will be presented, or "sold", to the network executives. It introduces major characters, sets the location, and gives the flavor of the series. Often the first episode of a series you see on television is not the pilot. The network may determine the concept of the pilot is good, but the first episode to be broadcast must grab the audience more than the pilot. So the pilot ends up being shown at a later time.

The writer of a pilot can expect to earn three times the fee for a single episode. He also receives royalties on each episode aired, plus a percentage of the profits. And, if he stays with the series as an associate producer or creative consultant, he can earn $5,000 per week or more. The incentives are substantial.

Credits for television programs always include a producer and a director. The producer is in charge of the series, from purchasing the scripts to getting the show on the air. He answers to the network executives. The director handles turning the script into film, working with actors on interpretation of lines and with cameramen on composing camera shots. A movie which lasts an hour and a half may take two months or more to film. A television series usually has to be filmed in one week, so the director doesn't have time to experiment with different angles or different deliveries of dialogue. This is why, in television, the camera directions in the script will generally be more detailed than in movies.

As a writer, you will not just jump into writing a script. There are certain steps which must be taken. First, there is the premise. This tells the basic idea for the teleplay. It is a synopsis in the fewest possible words, summarizing the main characters, the conflict, the opening scene, and how the conflict will be resolved.

The next step is the outline. In the television business, this is called the "treatment" and is the most important element of the teleplay, along with being the hardest to write. It takes the show, in a scene-by-scene narration, and describes the characters, scene locations, motivations, relationships, and summary of dialogue (although it contains no dialogue). It is the treatment which sells a producer on a new script or series, and what sells you as a writer.

A television drama is divided into acts. These acts are usually interrupted by commercials, putting another element of difficulty in their writing. Acts are composed of scenes, which are the basic units of television. You can think of a scene as being a segment of continuous action taking place in a single location. Changing a scene means setting up a new camera location.

The final step is setting down the dialogue in script format. Timing in television is critical. As harsh as it may sound, television programming is a vehicle for advertisers. With that in mind, the actual length of the script for a thirty minute series is only about 21 minutes and 45 seconds of story (ignoring opening and closing credits), which is usually split about in half for the first and second act.

The opening scene of a teleplay, called the teaser, should set the mood for the entire show and should introduce the viewer to the characters and conflict that are to follow. It is between one and two minutes and must grab the audience emotionally from the very first moment. The way to do this is through the use of dramatic action. Dramatic action equals emotional involvement. For instance, a child swimming at a beach is not dramatic action, but a child swimming at a beach with a shark lurking in the water nearby is dramatic action. This is a simple approach that worked quite well for a series of box office hits.

The structure of a television drama is similar to that of a novel, in that there is the presentation of the conflict, pursuit of conflict resolution, and climax, where the conflict is finally resolved. Because a television program is broken up by commercials, each act must function on its own. That is to say, each act must present a conflict which is partially resolved before the commercial break. In fact, to keep the story moving, each scene within each act should also have these elements. Every scene must work toward the goal of resolving the major conflict. Cause and effect interactions must be constant. You must know the climax before you start, and every scene must be written toward that ending.

Suspence is often used in television plotting. It helps prepare your viewer for the eventual climax. As an example, if a car's brakes are going to fail in the final scene, the viewer should see the brake lines leaking in a previous scene. Beware of introducing suspence that doesn't advance the plot. If the camera focuses on a revolver sitting on a table in the opening act, someone had better use the gun by the end of the story or your audience will feel cheated.

To break into television as a writer, you must produce a saleable script. It is easiest to write a script for a television series that already exists. You should select a series that has been on the air for more than a single season. The characters and locations are established for you and the more familiar you are with the series, the easier it will be to follow the current format.

Just as with a writer on assignment, you should go through all the steps outlined previously, including writing a premise and a treatment. Once you have your premise written and revised, show it to a relative or, better yet, present the idea verbally. Verbal presentation skills are frequently required in selling your idea to a producer. Listen to what your reviewers say. If one person does not like your idea, don't worry. But if ten different people tell you the idea is no good, you might want to take a hard look at your premise.

In producing true-to-life dialogue, it's frequently helpful to read the scene aloud. Remember, dialogue is written to be read. Use a partner to act out scenes. This is one form of brainstorming. Keep polishing until the scene flows like an effortless conversation.

Once you've completed and rewritten your script, you are ready for the second half of the job: selling your teleplay. Before you tackle this, you should register your script with the Writer's Guild of America, 8955 Beverly Blvd., Los Angeles, California 90048, Attn: Registration Department. This is similar to copyrighting a novel and, although it is not a guarantee against plagiarism, it does give you a certain amount of protection.

As a new television writer you will have to assume the function of agent, as well. To begin, you should contact anyone you know who might have ties to the television industry, no matter how remote. Tell these people you've written a script and ask them to read it and recommend anyone they might know who could help you sell it. If this doesn't produce any leads, the Writer's Guild publishes a monthly market newsletter and offers a list of approved agents, some of whom will accept new writers. Read the trade magazines of the television industry. "Variety" and the "Hollywood Reporter" frequently have information that can produce leads. As with writing and selling other forms of fiction, don't give up. Every professional television writer had to produce a first script. Those who are successful are the ones who stuck with it.

SCREEN PLAYS

If television is a slice of life, a movie is bigger than life. The screen play deals with themes on a grand scale. In fact, the entire movie process is one grand overstatement. Whereas a one-hour television drama may cost $100,000 to make, a one-and-one-half-hour movie may cost $10 million and often more. A dramatic series for television is taped and edited in one or two weeks. A movie often requires a year for completion. On television, actors are one-tenth actual size. In movies, they are ten to twenty times bigger than life.

A movie script, or screen play, combines character, theme, and plot but emphasizes only one. A disaster film fits into the last category.

The screen play is usually divided into three acts. The first act introduces the characters and establishes the conflict. The second act provides for intensification of the conflict to a crisis. And the final act reveals the resolution of the conflict.

Each act is divided into scenes. A scene is made up of all the dialogue and action relating to one location. The scene is further divided into shots. A shot is one camera setup. To keep the momentum of the film going, most scenes last two minutes or less. The audience will tend to lose interest if something major doesn't happen on screen at least every ten minutes.

A screen play starts out as a synopsis, which is a one or two paragraph summary of the plot.

The outline comes next and contains only the essential information about the characters and the plot. This will usually be seven to twelve typed pages.

The final stage before the actual scripting begins is the treatment. The treatment and the synopsis are usually the elements which an agent will use to sell your script, so they are as important as the actual screen play. The treatment is a fifteen to forty-five page detailed outline which describes the characters, settings, and specific action of the plot, and should include sample dialogue and possible camera shots. This is always written in present tense as if production is happening now.

Potential subjects for movies are bounded only by the writer's imagination. For a first screen play you might consider an adaptation from a book or stage play. Since stage plays usually only have three sets, the writer has the added challenge of creating additional settings for action.

Time plays an important part in the screen play. A theatrical plays deals with real time, but a movie can add dimension by dealing with the past, through flash-backs, and the future.

In your screen play you must grab the audience in the first minutes of your story. They are somewhat captive, but a slow start will set a slow pace for the rest of the picture. There are no commercial breaks or intermissions in movies to allow an audience to digest your meaning, so your character and plot development must be crystal clear. Remember that a movie is a visual medium. The pictures work with your words to communicate.

The director of a movie plays a different role from the director of a teleplay. The movie director has total control over the visual presentation of the script. The writer may make suggestions but, in the end, it is the director's job to interpret the script. For this reason, detailed camera directions are often not included in a screen play.

Movies are different from most other genre in that, in order to sell your script, you either need inside help or an agent. As in television, most studios will return unsolicited scripts unopened because of the numerous claims of plagiarism that are made against them. You can find the names and addresses of registered agents in your library. To start the ball rolling, send a letter of introduction, along with your synopsis and treatment to a number of different agents. The material you send must represent your best effort, as they will judge you on this. If your story interests them, or if they see potential in the way you put together your treatment, they may ask you to send copies of your script for their review. At that point, the agent would begin passing your script around to various producers, directors, studios, and actors. Few, if any, first-time screen plays are produced as is. Some are revised many times. Even if your agent doesn't think your story is producible, he may be impressed enough to get you an assignment from a studio.

The alternative to acquiring an agent is the inside track. If, as you wrote your script, you had a particular actor or actress in mind, send a copy of your synopsis and treatment to their agent. By the same token, if you have noted particular directors of movies you have seen, and you think your story is one a particular director might be interested in, send the synopsis and treatment to that director. Keep in mind that these people receive hundreds of unsolicited scripts and don't have time to give every inquiry detailed attention. Keep your letter brief and to the point and always include a self-address, stamped envelope for a response or the return of your material.

Even if you can't turn a sale from your first script, don't give up. You can't expect to learn everything about movie writing from your first experience. Most important, you must not sit back and wait while your script is circulating. Keep writing. After you have exhausted a reasonable number of alternatives, consider working with a local theater group to produce your screen play as a theatrical play. Once this has happened, you can put together a portfolio of the reviews and send those to some agents, showing them that your story did, indeed, have potential. The main thing is that you not give up.

Writing Exercises

Now that you have been introduced to the forms of fiction, it is time for you to make a decision as to which one is right for you. To help you realize the main differences, select an item from a newspaper which deals with action. This could be a traffic accident, a house fire, or even the birth of an animal at a zoo. Then, write a short one or two paragraph summary of how you would deal with this action for each of the six different genre: short story, novel (choose one of the sub-genres), children's fiction, theatrical play, teleplay, and screen play. From this you should be able to determine which genre you feel most comfortable working in and it may even provide the germ for an entire story.

3

Inspiration

By now you should have at least some idea as to which fictional genre you'll begin writing in. Now comes the hard part: the story.

The question most frequently asked of professional writers is, "Where do you get your ideas for stories?" The next most common question is, "What do you do when you get writer's block?" This chapter will address both of these important questions and offer some techniques to ensure you have plenty of the first and none of the second.

The Muses

The Greeks advanced much of what we accept today as culture, including sculpture, theater, and poetry. Not the least of what they left us were their religious beliefs, which we now term mythology.

The Muses were the nine daughters of Zeus and the Titaness Mnemosyne. By calling upon the Muses, man, who was tormented with grief and sorrow, could become relieved of his troubles. Through time, each Muse became associated with different areas of artistic endeavor: Clio became the Muse of history, Euterpe of lyric poetry, Thalia of comedy, Melpomene of tragedy, Terpsichore of dance, Erato of love poetry, Polyhymnia of songs to the gods, Urania of astonomy, and Calliope of epic poetry.

Many of the Greek tragedies begin with the author calling upon a Muse to guide the actors in their performance. Writers and artists throughout history have looked to the Muses for inspiration. Alas, you will notice, there is no Muse of fiction, so we must rely on other sources for inspiration.

Where Ideas Come From

Everyone has at least one novel already in their head. They have lived a story. The events that make up any person's life could easily be turned into a book-length manuscript. That would be an autobiography and in many cases would be less than interesting. However, as soon as the writer embellishes their life story, adding events that didn't happen and people who were never known, the story turns into fiction.

Other than a fictionalized autobiography, many would-be writers have a different story in their heads, one they have been mulling over for years and years. While driving long distances or just before falling asleep at night, chapter upon chapter has been created in the mind. Characters engage in a plot. Settings become crystal clear. Given an incentive and appropriate motivation, this writer would have little trouble turning these characters, who have been known for so long, into a manuscript.

Getting started on a first novel or short story is rarely a problem. Who knows where it comes from, but an idea bursts forth and the writer starts to write. Many writers never even considered writing until that first idea blossomed. Before the idea, there was no reason to write, so there was no concern about having nothing to write about. There was no void to fill. First efforts are written out of passion. It's not a job. The writer is not writing for money, at least to begin with. He is writing because he has a story straining to get out of his brain and onto the paper. Once that first story is finished, and worse if it's sold, the writer must decide whether to go on and write again or accept that he was only a one-story author and be satisfied with that. Some writers are satisfied with one triumph. But not the professional.

It is the second attempt at authorship which causes so much pain. Writers generally agree the most intimidating thing they face is a blank sheet of paper. The longer you look at it, the more it overpowers. You may have been thinking about the story idea for months, even written the opening paragraph in your head, time and again. However, the actual process of committing your words to paper, for some reason, is terrifying. Knowing the importance of the first sentence, some writers feel their words can't possibly be worthy. Some can't see the story beyond the first sentence. Writing careers have ended just because the writer-to-be couldn't bring himself to type out that ever-so-important first sentence. Knowing something of the thought process involved in creation can help you move forward.

Stories come from the same place as dreams: the deepest recesses of our minds. Dreams occur when the brain's memory cells are randomly activated. The reason this happens during sleep is because there is limited brain activity to interfer with the process. Science has determined that humans use only ten percent of their available brain while awake. The other ninety percent is filled with story ideas. In order to access those ideas, you must not let unproductive thought processes interfer.

These negative thought processes generally are self imposed and are brought about by stress or tension. Just as you can't force yourself to dream, you can't force yourself to come up with a good story idea. Comedians are frequently asked to say something funny on the spot. Taken unaware, the funny part of their brain seizes. They, themselves, will admit that they can't be "funny" on demand. The same is true for the writer. The moment you say to yourself, "I have to come up with a story idea," is the moment the vault doors slam shut on that important ninety percent of your brain. The more you want it, the less likely you'll be to get it. Panic will set in. Terror follows as you think you may have exhausted every possible idea in your head. Knowing the causes of this panic and how to deal with it is what separates the neophyte from the professional.

Fear of failure and the pressure to create often work together to produce "writer's block". This is an inaccurate, trendy idiom used by writers to explain away their inability to function as they would like to believe they are capable. All professional writers get this "ailment", it is said, so this somehow makes the "victim" seem more like a professional. The fact is, throwing your hand up to your forehead and proclaiming you are "blocked" is a certain indication of amateur standing. Believing that a professional writer can't write is as absurd as believing that a surgeon can't perform an operation or a garbage collector can't empty a trash can. If it is your job, if you are truly a professional, you write. Though you have no excuse to allow yourself to fall into the "writer's block" rut, there will be times, especially in the beginning, when, for one reason or another, you cannot bring yourself to put words on paper.

If a writer isn't writing, he's unemployed. Whatever the cause, there are several techniques professionals use to insure their continued ability to generate prose. This is a major area in the business of writing and you are encouraged to treat your creativity as you would your most precious writing tools. As every writer responds to different stimuli, not every technique will prove effective. This is by no means a comprehensive list.

Idea Generating Techniques

1. Look around.

Story ideas are all around you, you just have to train yourself to recognize them.

Whenever you are away from your writing area, don't think you're on vacation. The actual writing process is only a small part of being a writer. When you aren't writing, you must be preparing to write. That means carrying a pocket notebook with you all the time and using it to jot down little reminders of the characters you see and meet, action you observe, or places you visit.

For instance, while you are waiting for a bus (public transportation is a great way to encounter all types of different characters) take notice of the woman who waits next to you. Use all your senses and think about what she looks like, what makes her different from any other person. Notice her hair color and style. What kind of clothes does she wear? Does she smell of perfume? The sense of smell generates the greatest images. What does she do while she waits? Is she knitting? Reading a newspaper? Look at her hands. Listen as she asks the bus driver if he's going to her stop, even though she rides the same bus every day. Real characters make stories more interesting. Of course, you can't put real people in your stories, but every fictional character can benefit from elements derived from real people.

If you overhear two people arguing, listen to the exchange and analyze the dialogue. Think about how you would write such a scene in a story. Most arguments don't follow a logical sequence; most writing does.

Step into a library, a grocery store, or an old bank and breathe in. How would you describe the smells of these places? Cities smell different from rural areas. They also look different. Sunlight weaves its way through the buildings of a city, casting rectangular shadows. A farm field has thousands of little shadows that move constantly with shifting breezes.

Any one of these situations could spark an idea for a story. The key is in training yourself to use the inspiration that is all around you.

2. Look to your hobbies or job for story ideas.

One of the most natural sources of ideas for stories is something at which you are already an expert. Fishing, quilting, or butterfly collecting could easily suggest a direction for a story. An entire story could be built with an habitual gardener as the main character. Your job is another example of where your expertise can pay off. Give your main character your accounting job and see how he handles it. After-all, your characters can do things you would never dare.

3. Exercise your senses.

As a writer, you communicate through sensory images. In order for a reader to feel as if he knows the setting of your story, you must make him see, feel, hear, smell, and even taste. In order for you to communicate effectively, your own senses must be razor sharp.

Sitting at your typewriter or in an office all day dulls your senses: the same four walls, the same sounds, the same desk. Exercise your senses by going to a shopping mall, a zoo, or an amusement park. Even walking through a wooded park can help awaken your senses. Look, listen, and smell. Each new sensation will bring flashes of inspiration.

4. Exercise your imagination.

Children have active imaginations. They have no bounds separating reality from make-believe. As adults, we tend to overemphasize reality and repress our imaginations. Young people have no trouble making up stories, often on the spot. Some writers complain that, as children, they wrote voluminously, filling page after page with stories, poems, and songs, but as adults, they can't seem to come up with new ideas. It's not that they have run out of ideas, it's just that they have gotten out of the habit of imagining.

To revitalize your imagination, set aside some time and rekindle your childhood activities. Play games. Swing on a swing. Watch thirty minutes of cartoons on television. You have to work at retraining your brain to play make-believe. Having done this, you should not lack for story ideas.

Another way to work your imagination is to pick up a foreign magazine and make up stories to go with the pictures. This is an excellent exercise for your daily journal entry and can provide a wealth of new characters and situations.

5. Review your journal for story ideas.

Your journal should be the first place you look for story ideas. After all, that's one of the main reasons for keeping a journal. If you have kept your journal faithfully for several months, you should have a dozen or more good possibilities.

Your journal is also the place to look when you begin writing a difficult scene or about emotions you don't presently feel.

6. Start an idea file.

Ideas are not the same thing as plots. The "idea" is the spark that ignites the plot. It is the inspiration for the plot. You have to start with an idea and develop it into a story.

One of the best ways to make sure you never run out of ideas is to accumulate an idea file. Material for an idea file can come from newspapers and magazines, advertisements, or Christmas cards. Anything you come across that provides vivid images, or anything you think may have story potential, belongs in your idea file. Just as you write down ideas for characters and plots in your journal, you can collect ideas and organize them so they are accessible. These clippings can be kept in file folders and arranged by category so you don't have to shuffle through mounds of material for a character idea.

7. Let your characters speak to you.

Many writers talk about how the characters in their stories often take over the plot, causing totally unexpected turns. When you begin writing a story, you are just getting to know your characters. By the middle of the story, if you have done your job, your characters will be so well developed that their next move shouldn't be a mystery to you.

8. Write every day.

Just as a runner has to train his muscles, a writer has to train his brain. If writing is going to be your business, you must force yourself to work every day. Even on those days when you can't think of anything to write, sit at your desk and write your name over and over. You can't allow yourself to think you can take a day off just because you don't feel creative. That's too easy. One day off will turn into two, then into a week. Before you know it, a month will have passed and, if you do start writing again, you'll be starting from the beginning. You must allocate time to write. Once you get in the habit, you'll be uncomfortable when you aren't writing.

9. Break your routine.

The imagination responds to different stimuli. The same routine can sometimes lock up the thought process. So try something different. If you usually do your writing in the morning and you notice your productivity slipping, try writing in the evening. If you use a typewriter, try writing in longhand. Rearrange the furniture in your office. Even buying new shoes can be rejuvenating.

10. Read.

No one really knows what triggers the thought process. Sometimes ideas pop into our heads without any warning. What does seem to encourage our own thought process is continuous exposure to the written word. Whenever you aren't writing or observing, you should be reading. Poems, magazines, editorials, comics, and advertisements can all spark ideas. Thumb through the yellow pages of the telephone book. Browse through a dictionary. Often a single word or short phrase is all you need to get your story moving forward.

Inspiration from reading should naturally come as you are researching your story. For instance, reading about exotic locations will naturally suggest other elements which might be incorporated into your story.

11. Work at relaxing

There is no doubt that tension shuts off the flow of creativity. Trouble at your other job or aggravation at home can keep you from focusing on your writing. Yoga works for some. Exercise is also a good tension reliever.

Set aside some time when you can relax by yourself. Put soft music on the stereo, turn down the lights, and sit back in a comfortable chair. Close your eyes. Concentrate on relaxing each muscle in your body, starting with your head. Notice where your tongue is in your mouth. You are tense if your tongue is pressed hard against the roof of your mouth. Let it float. Notice how all the muscles in your face relax when you relax your tongue. Allow your arms and your legs to go limp. You should feel as if you are floating. Fill your mind with visions of clouds or a field of spring flowers. Imagine you are sitting beside a small stream and listening to the water trickle over little stones. Let your thoughts wander. Now you are on the way to opening the doors to your imagination.

You should get in the habit of keeping a pad of paper and a pencil next to your bed. You'll find many good ideas will come to you in the moments just before you fall asleep. This is a time when you are naturally relaxed. Also, make notes of your dreams. These totally uninhibited thoughts can often provide directions for plots and characters.

12. Don't worry about perfection.

Many writers begin with the fear of failing or of not being good enough. If you start with fear, you'll never progress. Accept that your first effort won't be perfect. That's what revision is for. Most authors revise a manuscript at least twice. Don't stuggle with a sentence in your head. Get it on paper now and worry about how it sounds later. Puzzling over a single sentence can bring an abrupt halt to your creative flow. Write it down and move on to the next. The same is true for the "right word". You can spend hours trying to think of the perfect word for a sentence, but that isn't writing. Leave a blank to fill in later, or use a word that's close. Make a note in the margin to think about the word at another time.

13. Use stream of consciousness.

Although stream of consciousness has no place in your story, it is a valuable technique for generating some good ideas. The way this works is you sit down at your desk and start writing down every thought that comes into your mind. The human mind works very fast, so you'll have to work to keep up. By recording every thought, you will undoubtedly jot down something that may have been so fleeting you would have missed it altogether otherwise. You may generate several pages of rubbish in a very short time but, if you even come up with one good idea, or even an interesting phrase, the effort will be rewarded.

14. Always have two writing projects in progress.

One of the best techniques for dealing with a lack of inspiration in a project is to have another project you can turn to. If you're working on a novel and your characters refuse to cooperate, start working on a short story or a non-fiction magazine article.

Sometimes, the best way to gain a new perspective on a story is to step away from it for a short time. You'll find that after a while away from your characters and your plot, you'll regain some of the enthusiasm you had when you began.

Switching writing projects is particularly good because it transforms the time you would waste waiting for inspiration into productive time. When you feel inspired for one project, attack it enthusiastically. If an idea pops into your head for another project, jump on it. This is how professional writers make the most efficient use of their time.

15. Know your first sentence before you start writing.

For many authors, the most stessful part of the day is winding a blank sheet of paper into the typewriter and hoping to be able to fill it with words. The very prospect of freezing is enough to keep the words from flowing.

To prevent this, always prepare in advance for the next day's work. The first sentence of the day is quite important. Stop in midparagraph, if necessary, and jot down some notes to help you get started the next time you sit down to write. In addition to providing a spring board for the next day, you will also benefit from thinking about that next sentence. After mulling it over for ten or twelve hours, it might even turn into the best sentence you write.

16. Write a letter.

If you aren't happy with the direction your story is taking, write a letter to an imaginary friend or to one of the characters in your story. Tell them what troubles you. Part of the problem-solving process is to make sure you know precisely what the problem is. It's surprising that writing down a problem often reveals a solution.

17. Take one step at a time.

One of the problems for new authors, especially at first, when they are bursting with enthusiasm for a project, is that they want to write the entire story all at once.

A novel-length story takes place over more than a moment in time. Days or months pass as the plot unfolds. As a writer, you can't expect to have the entire story conceived while you are still writing the first paragraph. This is what keeps some people from writing. They feel they can't start until they know every detail of how the story will end.

You will be happier with your progress if you divide a lengthy writing project into smaller pieces. Set your immediate goal as one chapter, not the entire novel. As you reach these goals, you'll feel a real sense of accomplishment.

18. Don't look to writers' groups for inspiration.

Most so-called ''writers' groups'' exist only to feed a writer's ego. At their meetings, the members stand around and compliment eachother on their unpublished works and gossip about those not in attendance. Not many story ideas or much inspiration come out of such social activities.

Remember, writing is largely an individual activity. Your best chance for success will be achieved by going it alone.

19. Don't acknowledge "writer's block".

If you tell yourself you have writer's block, you will have it. Your flow of words will dry up. However, if you recognize that there is no such thing as writer's block, you'll have no reason to stop writing. That's the most important lesson to be learned: no matter what, don't stop writing.

Writing Exercises

The nineteen techniques outlined above are not intended to be reserved for moments of crisis. These are methods you should be using every day. Reread the list and, in your journal, write a twentieth technique which you use or might use to help develop story ideas.

So you will start thinking in terms of exposition, pick out an inanimate object which you can see (a fire hydrant, a chimney, a stapler, etc.) and write at least two pages of detailed description. Include physical (size, shape, color) and, with the help of your imagination, intangible (history, how it's been used, who has owned it) descriptions. Instead of listing characteristics, focus on organizing the details so they flow smoothly.

4

Character Sculpting

It begins with a character, and once he stands up on his own feet and begins to move, all I can do is trot along behind him with a paper and pencil trying to keep up long enough to put down what he says and does.

William Faulkner

If you retain nothing else from this book, remember this: fiction is characters. It's not plot or theme, though these are essential elements, but characters without which a work of fiction could not exist. Characters breathe life into your prose, conveying your message. Take away the characters and your story becomes barren. Characters are the story.

Given the supreme importance of characters, this chapter will help you invent characters your readers will want to know about, give your characters a reason for living, and flesh out their skeletons to make them as real as they can possibly seem. You will learn that characters are three-dimensional entities which must virtually leap off the page into your reader's lap.

Many first-time authors make the mistake of describing their characters through paragraph after paragraph of narration. In real life, when you meet someone, you don't spend the first ten minutes after the introduction analyzing every detail of that person. You don't, at the first instant, know that person's life story. What you may do is strike up a conversation. They tell you about themselves and you tell them about yourself. Take note: the characters are telling the story. In fiction writing, there is an ever-present temptation to take the story-telling ability away from the characters and put it in the hands of the author. The characters, not the author, through their dialogue, thoughts, and actions, tell the story. The author must step back and let the characters do their work.

Character Types

Many different instruments comprise a symphony orchestra: violins, drums, trumpets, flutes, oboes, etc. All these instruments work together to make the orchestra interesting. Few would pay the price of a concert ticket to hear sixty bassoons.

The instruments of your story are characters. And, like the composer, you must provide a variety to hold your readers' interest. In addition to making your story interesting, character variety helps a reader keep the players straight. If every character differed only in name, even the writer would have trouble remembering who was whom.

It's not a crime for a writer to include himself as a character in his story. This is only natural, since the writer may know himself better than any character he could conceive. However, refrain from making every character think and act the same as you. It wouldn't happen in real life and it shouldn't happen in your story.

Just as every instrument in an orchestra has a name, every character type can be broadly classified.

Cowards are a universal type of character. Everyone is afraid of something, but a true coward will put his fears ahead of all else. Most often, the coward's fears are unfounded. There is a fine line, however, between cowardice and caution. Fear of death from engaging in a military battle would be deemed cowardly by a general, but a reasonable response by many others.

Bullies are more than big kids picking on little kids. The bully character knows no age limits and his abuse isn't strictly physical. Any character with power can intimidate others. A slum lord can bully tenants. A foreman can bully a new employee. The key to a bully's success is that no one will stand up to him. Usually this proves to be his undoing.

Teachers are frequent character types in fiction. This is not limited to school teachers, but includes any character who helps another learn. The teacher character need not be formally educated. Any experienced person can teach the lessons of life.

The character of a reactionary doesn't act, he reacts. These are the characters who think they are advancing a movement when they are really halting forward progress. They will act without assessing the consequences. Members of activist groups are often lumped into this category, sometimes incorrectly. An activist becomes a reactionary when he allows personal biases to dictate the actions of a group.

Villains in modern fiction can be complex. Rarely is a villain all bad. By the same token, heros are never perfect.

Show-offs always want the spotlight on them, no matter the risk. They will attempt any number of foolhearty activities to insure they remain at the center of attention. This isn't limited to the attention of a group. A show-off may only be vying for the attention of a member of the opposite sex.

Vigilantes aren't restricted to the old west and aren't always trying to hang someone. Vigilantes so strongly believe they are right, they will stop at nothing to enforce their beliefs.

The list could go on indefinately. There are dozens of character types. Just look around and you'll realize that in life, as in fiction, no two people are alike. In a room filled with thirty people, each will have a distinctive personality. You may not even find two people you could classify as the same "type". This variety of character type is what makes fiction interesting.

To enhance the effect of different characters, try using contrast. Man/woman, meek/loud, rich/poor, country/city, old/young, educated/uneducated, honest/con-artist, social clout/peasant: these opposite pairs work together to provide greater impact than the two types used independently. Comedy teams have used this technique since before the days of Laurel and Hardy and Burns and Allen.

Beware of character cliches, like the little old lady. These characters have been so over used that they distance themselves from reality. Your reader has seen the same character used so often that they become distracted from your story. If you must use a frail, elderly woman, make her unique by giving her at least one characteristic the reader would not expect.

Casting Characters

Your next question might very well be, "Where do I get the ideas for characters?"

By now you should be able to anticipate the answer: your journal.

Characters enter the writer's life via two avenues: characters that are real and characters born from our imagination.

Real characters are encountered every day as we go about our lives. We pass them on the street, sit behind them in restaurants, and bump into them on elevators. As a fiction writer, you must be on the lookout continuously for characters. Your pocket notebook will be your ally. Whenever you happen upon an interesting person, make notes and further develop them in your journal. Friends, relatives, and people you work with may be sources of character material. The problem with real characters is you can't use them in a fictional story. Privacy laws protect real people from having their personal lives made public without their consent. We can't, however, ignore real people altogether.

Imaginary characters all have their basis in fact. Every fictional character has at least one element which was derived from a real person. Although you can't use your next door neighbor in a story, you can create a character based on your neighbor. The name would have to be different. Instead of obese, he might be thin. Your neighbor has brown hair, so give your character red hair. Change the number of children, the name of his dog, the temperment of his wife, and the city where he lives. A character is born.

Aside from neighbors and people close to you, other places to look for characters include newspapers, magazines, television shows, movies, and books. Of course, you can't copy these characters directly, but you can use these sources for inspiration; a starting point.

Character Mapping

Alternately, this section might be called "Know Your Characters", because if you don't know them, your readers will never know them, either. To develop a character to its fullest you must get into his head and become that character.

The 2-page "Character Map" which follows is a way for you to get to know the characters in your story. It will guide you in developing a full biography of your characters. You must know far more about them than you would put in a story. For them to seem real, you must gather as many details of their lives as possible. Treat this as an interview, where you answer for your characters. Remember, character mapping is for the author. Your reader doesn't want all the information about the characters, only that which advances the story. As a general rule, consider that your character should reveal no more of himself to your reader than your reader, in the same situation, might be able to learn on his own.

The first step in bringing a character to life is a name. Charles Dickens was the master of descriptive naming. You knew what his characters were all about the moment you met them. No one could have any doubts as to the character of Ebenezer Scrooge or Mr. Gradgrind.

Today, relying too heavily on a name can turn into a cliche. The exception to this is in juvenile fiction, where Mr. Miser can be used to teach a concept. Otherwise, real people must have real names. That's not to say names can be boring. Tom is a simple name, boring for a fictional character unless he is simple by nature. Tommy is the name of a little boy. Thomas is highbrow. A name should work subtly to

Character Map

Name: a.k.a.:

Birthdate: Birthplace: Age:

Currently Resides:

Marital Status:

Physical Characteristics:

Education:

Family:

Pets:

Special Friends:

Social Interaction:

Significant Past:

Habits:

Character Map

Name: a.k.a.:

Speech:

Work:

Hobbies:

Politics:

Religion:

Likes:

Dislikes:

Philosophy of Life:

Motivation:

provide the reader with information about your characters. Alternately, you may want to use irony in naming characters: simple names for complex characters and complicated names for simple characters. Spend time and put thought into developing names.

Aside from your character's given name, include what he is called by others: his also known as (a.k.a.) or nickname. This can be a pet name used by a lover, a churlish name used by a rival, or a name that somehow portrays the character's personality. A nickname gives you an opportunity to add depth to your character and to the relationships in which he's involved.

The next step in bringing characters to life is a birthdate and place. The one date everyone remembers is their own birthday. It has a personal importance for real people and for fictional characters, as well. Birthdates are compared and exchanged in social situations and can be used by you to show how your characters feel about their age: being young or growing older. For the writer, the birthdate tells the era during which the character grew up. People who lived during the Depression have values different from Baby-boomers. Characters who experienced World War II view the act of war differently from those who lived through the Vietnam War. Think about how events which occurred during your character's life may have left lasting impressions.

The place of one's birth is basic to understanding them. People reared in different parts of the country behave very differently from one another. The place of a person's origin often determines mannerisms and speech patterns. Variations occur even within geographical locales. City dwellers see life differently from those brought up in a rural setting. If you know where your characters grew up, you'll have an insight into their personal philosophy.

During their lifetimes, most people move several times so it's important to include your character's present location. More than city and state, you need to determine whether he lives in a house, an apartment, or on a park bench. Does he live alone or with parents or a spouse? What's his house like? Big? Small? Palatial? A mess?

Is your character married, single, divorced, or widowed? All this impacts how your characters will go about their everyday lives.

To the reader, what your character looks like is generally less important than how he acts. For consistency, though, you must be able to visualize your character down to his freckles. Your readers will see your characters as they want. You could describe someone as tall and dark, and your readers might interpret, from other cues, short and fair. No matter how hard you work to give your readers a complete picture of a character, they will always come up with their own image. Just as you created the character from someone you knew, your readers will interpret your character based on someone they have known. This is natural, so don't fight it. Give your reader essential description and let him fill in the rest. If you provide too much description your reader will become confused. It is best to present physical characteristics one at a time, building the character as a sculptor molds a statue.

Your characters may be college educated, may have only completed high school, or may be self-educated. In addition to formal education, which may or may not tell anything about your character, you should describe in your Character Map where he learned the lessons of life. Is he the product of caring parents or a grandparent? Did he learn everything he knows on the street, where he had to learn in order to survive? Or was there a kindly mentor in his past? Maybe your character has yet to experience life. Sometimes this latter education tells more about how a character acts and reacts.

Family, pets, and special friends: their existence is less important than how your character feels about them. Is he close to his family or do they no longer speak? How does he treat animals? If he treats a dumb animal kindly and with patience, he's probably a decent human being. Kicking puppies shows a lack of maturity as well as compassion. Does he have close friends for whom he would do anything, or is he totally self-absorbed?

How does your character act at social gatherings? Is he an introvert or extrovert? Is he a smooth talker, covering hidden insecurity? He could be a social climber or might avoid crowds altogether. Think about how he or she will interact with members of the opposite sex.

What is important in your character's past? The past, in part, determines what is important in the present. Does your character continually focus on the past? Is there something in his past he is trying to forget? A woman? An accident? Does he use the past as a lesson for the future? Revealing a character's past can be difficult. Rarely, as in real life, will someone volunteer information about a painful past. Frequently this has to be drawn out by another character. A mysterious past, created by revealing fragments of a sordid history over the course of the story, creates suspence and will keep your readers interested.

What habits does your character have which tell about his personality? Does he have nervous habits? Nail biting? Chain smoking? How about compulsive habits? Constantly tidying? Excessive personal hygiene? What are his vices? Virtues? Don't fabricate habits just to fill the page. Habits should be used to tell something about your characters or to distinguish one character from another.

Speech is usually a function of where your character grew up, both geographically and socioeconomically (further discussed in Chapter 6). When writing dialogue, you'll have to concentrate on your character's speech so you don't introduce elements which don't belong. What figures of speech would your character use repeatedly? This is a good way of providing continuity of character. Does your character speak in short sentences or long ones? Does he think before he speaks, or is he constantly putting his foot in his mouth?

Everyone works and everyone has a hobby. Determine how your character feels toward his job. How does he approach his job? With enthusiasm or indifference? Does he hate his job? If so, why? Does he show exceptional skill in his work? Is he the most talented but the least rewarded? How does he get along with his boss and co-workers? Does he think he could run the business better than his boss? Where is he in the business pecking order? Better yet, where does he place himself? Is he a team player or strictly a one-man show?

What importance does your character place on his leisure time? The rewards of a hobby are personal rather than financial, so a hobby shows what is important to your character when he is on his own time. Does he use this time to better himself through artistic endeavors or night school? Or does he swill beer and watch television? Taxidermy may be a revealing hobby. Here is an opportunity to introduce opposites. A burly construction worker who collects butterflies has the potential to be an interesting character.

Politics and religion: it is important to know where your character stands on these volatile issues. More important than what political party he belongs to or what specific religion he practices, is whether he takes an active part in politics and whether he is naturally religious. You can still believe in God without going to church. By the same token, just because your character is a deacon, he is not necessarily a saint. Generally, politics and religion make strange bedfellows. A minister who runs for public office would certainly be a memorable character.

Likes and dislikes are personal preferences which further classify your character and make him an individual. These can include areas such as music, food, types of people, art, furniture, or colors.

The final two categories on the Character Map have major importance. Every thought your characters have and every action they undertake is determined by their philosophy of life and their motivation.

A philosophy of life is the basic principle your character lives by. These beliefs are so deeply rooted in an individual that they don't often change over time. He may believe that nice guys finish last, so he strives to be tough, may hold truth and honor above all else, may live by "an eye for an eye", or may believe his purpose on earth is to help others. There are as many of these principles to live by as there are different characters. Don't expect this to come to you easily. You have probably spent a lifetime coming up with your own philosophy of life.

Motivation, which is dealt with in more detail later in this chapter, is a short term inner drive which directly causes a character to take action. Motivations last only until the desire is realized and may change during the course of your story. Money, status, love, and jealousy are only a few of the many driving forces which motivate characters.

Only after you have completed a Character Map for each of your characters, having stepped into their minds and discovered what they are all about, are you ready to start writing your story. Non-fiction writing requires extensive research. Writing fiction requires researching your characters to the same extent. As you write, you should refer to your Character Map frequently for direction as to what your characters will do and say, so keep it close at hand. Characters in your story, like real people, grow over time, so you may find yourself changing your Character Map as your story grows. Logic dictates that you make no change in character traits without considering the total picture. Radical changes only occur in real life in response to exceptional forces.

Point Of View

In fiction, from whose point of view the story is told is of major importance. Think of it as a camera planted in the head of a character and focusing through that character's eyes. The reader sees what the character sees and knows what this character is thinking. The camera, however, cannot record other characters' thoughts.

As an example, your point-of-view character may enter a room of several people. Your character's thoughts about the room and the people in it are revealed to the reader. A woman steps over to your character and speaks. Your character speaks and thinks some more. We never know what the woman is thinking, only what she says. How she speaks may give away her thoughts but we can't see inside her head.

Many beginning authors make the mistake of using an omniscient point of view, where thoughts of every character are revealed simultaneously. He said, he thought, she said, she thought only serves to confuse the reader. This doesn't mean that the thoughts of other characters can't be revealed through other means, like dialogue, or that you are limited to only one point of view through the entire story.

The point of view can, and should, change throughout your story. In one chapter you can tell the story through the eyes of the heroine. In the next chapter the camera can move into the head of the villain. This way the reader will get the whole story. You should, however, be careful not to change the point of view within a chapter. This will cause your reader to pause and ask himself, "What's going on?".

Stories told in the first person can have only one point of view.

Through the entirety we only see what the storyteller sees and know what the storyteller thinks. The thoughts of other characters must remain a mystery. The main problem with a story told in first person, aside from potential boredom, is that your main character must be present in every scene. Nothing can happen without him in the room. The tendancy is for this type of story to seem biased, as if the reader is only getting one side of a multi-sided story.

Motivation

Exciting characters think, talk, and act. Each thought, every word, and every action is brought about in response to something: motivation.

In real life, actions don't always make sense, but in fiction the author must provide sense even for senseless actions.

There are three types of motivating factors which can occur in a story.

First, there is the motivation which needs little or no explanation. These are factors which are obvious to the reader and make complete sense; the type of motivation which the reader, himself, has experienced. A parent who risks his life to save his child is a strong motive which doesn't need to be explained. A man traveling long distances to find his lost love is another example.

Next, there are actions which seem out of character. Without explanation, this type of action would appear to be a mistake to your reader. A reader may not accept that, having always stirred his coffee with a spoon, your character suddenly switches to using his finger. To satisfy the reader, you need only show that the character believed the spoon provided with his coffee had poison on it.

Finally, there are those actions which are totally unbelievable. The reader won't believe a particular character would behave in a specific manner. This type of motivation requires the author to tell the reader what went before to cause the character's action. The writer must provide justification to satisfy the reader. For instance, a charac-ter of mild manner may commit murder if he is pressured past his breaking point. Make certain the reader knows the source of that pressure.

Motivation is complex and can change during the course of a story. A villain is not motivated only by evil. His evil actions are the result of other motivating factors, like a childhood of abuse. Changes are always the result of actions. A character does not suddenly realize the errors of his ways and change into a different person. These changes happen over time.

As you write, you must continually ask yourself why your characters are acting the way they are. If you can't answer, your characters lack motivation.

Writing Exercises

In order for you to become familiar with the process, complete a Character Map using yourself as the subject. You don't necessarily have to stick strictly to the truth, but you must be complete.

Write a scene in which two characters meet and exchange dialogue. Begin by deciding on the characters and completing a Character Map for each. Provide a setting, but don't use any narration. Let your characters do all the work. In the course of their conversation you must convey essential physical characteristics, what kind of personalities they have, what they do for a living, and something about their past. In short, you should help your reader get to know your characters. Remember, use no narration, only dialogue.

5

Plot Development

If the characters are the building blocks of fiction, then the plot is the framework upon which the blocks are laid.

Looked at in a different way, the plot is like providing your reader with stones to step on to cross a river. Crossing the river is the challenge and each stone moves the reader closer to his goal. A stone that is more than a step away from the previous stone must be bridged. Any stone that sends the reader backward must be eliminated.

The purpose of this chapter is to introduce the different types of dramatic plots and the elememts which comprise them, and offer techniques for creating a successful plot.

A Pattern Of Cause And Effect

In addition to being a philosopher, biologist, moralist, and political thinker, Aristotle (B.C. 384-322) was the founder of literary criticism. He wrote that plot is an imitation of action and that, taken as a whole, the structure must be such that if one part is removed, the whole will be disjointed.

In short, a plot is a pattern of cause and effect, where one event brings about another, directing the story toward its end.

Aristotle was the first one to reduce plotting to a formula. The five elements of the Aristotelian plot are:

1. Establish situation - characters are defined and placed in a relationship. The characters are supplied with a goal.

2. Rising action - the goal is pursued, but not without conflict.

3. Reversal of situation - an event, a surprise, or a crisis occurs which at first may seem normal but which later proves to be disastrous.

4. Reappraisal - the characters become aware of the changes. Today this would be called the climax.

5. Falling action - the events which lead to the final resolution.

In Aristotle's formula, the reversal of situation was always brought about through fate and the falling action in a tragedy always had catastrophic results: the heroine typically died. With minor variation, the Aristotelian plot has survived for more than two thousand years.

Story Lines

The story line is the plot expressed in the fewest possible words. For instance:

Woman falls in love with man; old boyfriend tries to break up romance; new boyfriend triumphs over old boyfriend.

Another might be:

Man goes into jungle to find lost missionaries; man becomes lost, himself; man encounters dangerous wild-life and hostile natives; man befriends natives and rescues missionaries.

These story lines are the very beginning of a story idea, the bare bones to which the author will add flesh to make the story come alive. Notice, however, that even these simple statements have the essential elements of the classic plot. Each introduces characters and presents them with a goal. Their ability to achieve their goal is hindered, though not by fate. Finally, their goal is realized.

Around the turn of the century, Georges Polti, a dramatic critic, wrote a treatise titled "The Thirty-six Dramatic Situations" in which he proposed that every dramatic story ever written could be reduced to one of his numbered story lines. His premise is largely correct, but Polti mistakenly identified story elements as story lines. For instance, one of Polti's dramatic situations is "Murder". By itself, murder is not a situation, though it may be a key element in bringing about a dramatic situation.

It is important to remember that plot is built upon trouble. The trouble of others is interesting: it sells newspapers and it sells fiction. A story without conflict, without crisis, won't sell. Even fairy tales have crisis. A fictional crisis may develop in the rising action from elements which, by themselves, are insignificant but when brought together produce a crisis. For example, consider our jungle story from above. A dead tree limb dangling above the jungle floor is insignificant. Add to this that the jungle floor is composed of quick sand and we are little closer to a crisis situation. However, place your hero in the jungle, being persued by a lion and a crisis begins to form. If the hero, in running from the lion, falls into the quick sand and grabs the tree limb, only to have it crumble in his hand, a full-blown crisis has blossomed.

A plot must also have cause and effect relationships. Fate doesn't work in modern fiction. The author must constantly make the reader believe the actions of his characters are true-to-life. Chance happenings, such as an incriminating letter falling out of a desk; a character picking up a telephone for no reason, only to overhear another character plotting a murder; or a penniless hero finding a large sum of cash on the street signal a weak plot. Coincidence can destroy your credibility as a writer.

This isn't to say that your character can't find a letter in a desk, but he must have a reason for looking through the desk. Maybe he's searching for a pen to write a telephone message. Every action your characters take must have a cause.

A Beginning, Middle, And End

There are two basic forms for fictional plots: chronological plots and developed plots.

The simplest form of story portrays the adventures of a single character, written in the order the events occur. This is basically the form taken in DeFoe's ''Robinson Crusoe'' and is an example of chronological plotting. These stories take place in the present time, one action following another. Although it would seem the most simple, chronological plotting is often the most difficult. Similar to the story told in the first person, the strict chonological plot must stick to the present. The author must not write in the past or foretell future actions. In addition, it's impossible to give simulanteous accounts of events which happen at the same time.

More complex stories involve many characters, each with significant importance. Instead of moving forward in a straight line, the developed plot may take many twists and turns. Unlike the chronological plot, the developed plot may, in the beginning, allude to the ending. That is, the reader may, from information provided by the author, know ahead of time how the story will end. This information can be presented in the form of flash-backs. It is not necessary that the structure of events occur as it would in the real world. In fiction, the actions of the characters are purposely manipulated by the storyteller.

Regardless of the plotting method you choose, your story must have a beginning, middle, and end.

The beginning sets the scene, introduces the characters, establishes the point-of-view, gives essential background about the problem the character will face, and arouses the reader's interest. It is important to establish the problem early in your story. The sooner your reader becomes involved in other people's problems, the better your chance for holding his attention.

One proven method for grabbing reader attention is through the use of a narrative hook. Here, the writer uses a character or prop to tease the reader. You could "hook" a reader by having a character notice a handgun on a night stand which might be used to commit a crime. Or a young female character might complain of a stomach-ache only to have the reader infer she may be pregnant. A word of caution: don't introduce elements which have no bearing on the story. Readers enjoy being teased but don't like to be tricked. If there is a gun in the first chapter of your story, someone must make use of it before the end.

As a way of introducing the conflict, give your reader some history about how the conflict came to be. Since your story is told in the past tense, use the past perfect tense (had said) to let your reader know what went on before.

The middle of the story should focus on the presentation of complications and the factors which contributed to them. Keep reminding your reader of the character's ultimate goal and throwing roadblocks to stop forward progress. A good rule-of-thumb is to have your protagonist make three attempts to solve the problem, only to be set back by a failure each time. Less than three and your reader will believe your character isn't making an honest effort; more than three and the problem becomes unresolvable. Each attempt should bring your character closer to success.

By the end of the middle, your character must make an agonizing decision which will point the way to the solution. This is the crisis, the point where all appears lost and a monumental decision must be made. This could take the form of your hero giving up all efforts to maintain personal wealth in order to gain the love and respect of a woman.

The end of the plot is the climax of your story. The problem is solved. This is the denouement (literal translation; untying), where everything becomes clear to your character. Resist the temptation to dwell on the ending. When the action peaks, the story is over. Provide only as much explanation as is necessary to make your ending believable and to satisfy the reader. Remember, trouble is what holds your reader's interest. After the trouble is over, the reader wants to move onto someone else's distress.

Plot Outlines, Pyramids, And Flowcharts

The elements of a plot path are (1) hero, (2) goal, and (3) obstacles. Write these down and stick them to the wall in front of your typewriter. Commit them to memory. With these all-important three, you have the makings of a story someone will read.

If fiction writing were nothing more than remembering hero, goal, and obstacles, your job would be easy. Afterall, you not only want readers, you want paying readers. So you have to put more in your plot: you have to develop it.

Plot development is one of the most analyzed areas of writing. Scholars especially like to take apart a story and reduce it to its bare essence. Various writers have created pyramids and graphs to show the rise and fall of action in a story, exhorting authors to merely follow their formula for guaranteed success. Once again, if it were that easy, everyone would be a successful author. These formulas are really nothing more than a restatement of the Aristotelian plot: establish a situation and a goal, create complications which lead to a crisis, and resolve the problem to accomplish the goal.

One of the best tools, in fact an essential tool, for helping the writer develop a plot is the plot outline or flowchart. You may complain that an outline will stiffle your creativity or that you will allow your characters to dictate the story's direction. These are excuses of the lazy writer. Understand that no plot outline is cast in stone. The purpose of setting your plot into an outline format is to help you. In fact, few successful authors could write a novel-length manuscript without some sort of outline to guide their hand.

The simplest plot outline should include:

I. The introduction of the characters and the conflict.

II. Deepening of oppositions.

III. Point of crisis.

IV. Resolution of conflict.

The first item in the outline is pretty clearcut. Setting the scene, introducing characters, establishing your conflict, and presenting background material are elements which must appear in your first chapter. There is little flexibility here. Remember that in your introduction you should introduce alternatives for your characters to follow in the pursuit of the conflict resolution.

In order for your plot to develop, the obstacles which block your character from achieving his goal must grow. This is the area where the true master storytellers excel. Drama hinges on disruption. Just when your reader thinks the goal is in reach, you pull it away from your character. If you keep your character trying, your readers will follow along.

One of the keys to creating a dramatic situation is taking something and putting it where it doesn't belong. Uproot your characters and put them in an unfamiliar setting. A young woman with a flat tire isn't particularly dramatic, but give her that flat tire on a deserted street at midnight and the potential for trouble arises.

If you don't want your character seeking trouble, then trouble must come to him. This is the premise of the movie chase scene, where the innocent hero is trying to evade antagonists.

Plots evolve from the strengths and weaknesses of your characters. No character is perfect. The challenges they face are tests of their character.

The point of crisis comes toward the end of your story when the oppositions can no longer exist together. It's where two trains, shrouded in fog and heading toward eachother at full speed on the same track, thunder onto a trestle four-hundred feet above a rocky gorge. It's the point in the story when something must happen. The forces driving your story can't continue as they are. At this point, a normal person would give up and succumb. But not you character.

Resolving crises is an area where we can learn from the early movie makers. "Cliff hangers" were stories with multiple crisis/climax segments which occurred over several episodes. One episode would end with Nellie tied to a train track, a locomotive speeding toward her. The following installment would resolve the previous crisis by having the hero untie Nellie and pull her from the track just as the train came thundering by. This crisis behind them, Nellie would fall into another predicament only to be rescued in the next episode. Audiences would return time and again to discover what kind of trouble awaited Nellie. Other people's trouble is interesting.

Your first attempt at an outline will probably produce less than a single sheet and contain only the key elements of your story. Think of it as telling the entire story to a friend. Because of time constraints, you would have to leave the details until another time.

Keep this first draft handy. As you think of additional characters or situations which would enhance the conflict, add them to the outline. At this developmental stage, any idea is worth writing down. Later, it may seem silly, or it may spark a better idea. In its near final form (an outline is never finished until the manuscript is complete), your outline may be several pages in length and read much like a short story. Remember, though, only essential elements belong in an outline. A paragraph describing a location should be reserved for the actual story. Limit such a description to one or two words in your outline.

Fleshing Out The Story Line

One of the most difficult tasks to master in fiction writing is pacing. The difference between fiction and real life is that in real life, action isn't constant. In your own life, there are times when nothing is happening to you. In fiction, if nothing is happening to your characters, you are going to lose your readers. This is where pacing comes into play.

In your story, you want to stress the active elements and ignore those times when the action is slack. Provide your characters with emotional ups and downs.

Another skill that's important in fiction writing is the ability to get the most from every scene you write. Some refer to this as milking a scene, but you have to remember that life does not happen suddenly, it emerges over time. A rose blossom unfolds so slowly that its action is almost imperceptible. Love starts out slowly and builds. The same is important in fiction. You don't want to rush through important scenes. Use delaying tactics to postpone a scene's climax. (Just as the story has a climax, or peak, every scene should achieve a little peak.) Build tension in your reader by giving him hints of what is to come. Provide bits of information, a little at a time, always dangling a carrot in front of your reader to keep him wanting to know more.

Variations of the developed plot include double plots, the use of mystery, and surprise endings.

The double plot combines two different stories which complement one another. This gives the author an opportunity to exploit a theme from two different angles. Here, a plot flowchart is essential to keep the writer clear on the development of the action.

The use of "mystery" is a technique which will also keep the reader turning pages. Mystery involves providing your reader with information that raises the question, "Why?," while withholding certain information that would answer that question. You must never conceal information for the sole purpose of being mysterious, and you should never use mystery that does not add to the unfolding of the plot.

A surprise ending or a "twist" provides high levels of entertainment value, while showcasing a writer's skill. Stephen King is a master of the surprise ending, as shown in the film adaptation of his novel, "Carrie." In the final scene, when you think the action is over and you are breathing a sigh of relief, the sole survivor of a prom-night massacre lies in a hospital bed, teetering on the edge of consciousness. She dreams she is placing a bouquet of flowers on Carrie's grave, the house which Carrie brought down upon herself. Suddenly, the arm of a corpse erupts from the rubble, grabbing the girl's arm, and pulling her into the grave. A powerful ending leaves a lasting impression.

Writing Exercises

Choose one of the two story lines on pages 72 and 73 and develop it into a two-page plot outline. Make sure you include: your main characters and how you will introduce them, the conflict and what oppositions will be met in resolving the conflict, what will bring about the point of crisis, and how your character will solve his problem.

Alternately, make up your own story line and develop it into a two-page plot outline. In this first attempt, keep the story line simple so you can concentrate on the major plotting elements. As you improve your plotting skills you can focus on increasingly complex plots.

6

Dialogue and Narration

The author of fiction has two options available for conveying his story: dialogue and narration.

Through dialogue, the characters tell the story as they talk to other characters and to themselves. With narration, the author tells the story. Good fiction writing is always a combination of dialogue and narration in varying proportions.

Reasons For Dialogue

The proper use of dialogue in a story is a skill a writer learns, just as he learns proper sentence structure. Dialogue adds immediacy and depth to your story, but its improper usage can kill an otherwise decent work of fiction. The key to understanding these differences lies in knowing why writers use dialogue.

There are three main objectives which dialogue seeks to accomplish: (1) show character, (2) further action, and (3) convey information.

How your characters speak is important in making them come alive for your readers. Dialogue puts your reader in the scene, eavesdropping on your characters. It tells the reader where the character came from, the extent of their education, and distinguishes one character from another.

It is important to develop your characters completely before you start putting words in their mouths, otherwise there is a tendency for them all to sound like the author and to talk alike. As part of your Character Map you should include details about how your characters talk and phrases which are unique to them. Emotions are transmitted through dialogue, so don't tell what your characters are feeling, let them say it for themselves. Use dialogue to clarify a character's traits, goals, and desires. And, since no one stands perfectly still while speaking, describe the gestures and actions your characters use as they speak.

Dialogue is action. When two people are engaged in conversation, something is happening. Consider this: a reader will stop reading and put the book down in the middle of narration but not in the middle of dialogue. Dialogue involves the reader to such an extent that he simply must know how the exchange ends.

Remember, though, a character must have a reason for speaking. One of the best ways to show friction between two characters is by engaging them in a heated conversation. Dialogue must always advance the story and, so, must always be associated with action. Action frequently draws dialogue out of a character as when they respond verbally to some event. Even when a character talks to himself there must have been some action which drew the words out of him.

An interesting way to convey information is through conversation. Narration conveys the story indirectly. The reader has to accept what the storyteller says. Dialogue, on the other hand, conveys the story directly, putting the reader right in the middle of the action. In this information mode, there is sometimes a tendency to make the dialogue seem unnatural or to turn it into a monologue. When a character makes a long speech, he leaves the realm of dialogue and begins a narration. Although this is acceptable, you shouldn't overuse it. Also, the dialogue can only convey information which would naturally be known to the speaker. If you are using an omniscient point-of-view, only the storyteller will know everything. You must beware of giving your characters supernatural powers.

There are two other reasons why writers use dialogue which have nothing to do with advancing the story, but are worth mentioning, just the same.

Dialogue has the ability to entertain your readers. Humans communicate through conversation. We like to hear other people talk. It gives us a sense of being part of what's happening; being in the conversation. The entertainment value of dialogue, however, must not overshadow the work the dialogue must accomplish.

Dialogue also serves to break up narration. This may seem trivial, but it actually helps sell books. When a potential buyer picks up a book and flips through the pages, subconsciously he will be taken aback by page after page of long, uninterrupted paragraphs. Shorter paragraphs are much more inviting. Short paragraphs broken up by dialogue are even more inviting.

A Delicate Balance

If a little dialogue is good, then a lot of dialogue must be really good, right?

Wrong. Although a story without any dialogue will seem superficial and lifeless, too much dialogue can slow the pace. In-depth conversations rarely occur during times of intense action. One paragraph of narration can provide more information than a page of dialogue, so it's important not to let long sections of dialogue slow the forward progress of your story.

There are no set rules to follow to determine the proper proportion of dialogue and narration. You have to include just enough variety to make reading interesting.

Romances are built on emotion and nothing can portray emotions better than dialogue. In this type of story the reader wants to overhear what the characters say. Romance readers thrive on being privy to intimate conversations.

Adventure stories, on the other hand, should be packed with action and, therefore, require less dialogue and more narration. Fast-paced stories, with heroes chasing through the jungle or heroines being pursued by scoundrels, can get bogged down with too much dialogue. Here, your goal should not be to break up narration with dialogue, but to make sure your dialogue is broken up with sufficient narration. A character might speak to another and engage in action before receiving a response.

Narration is no less important to your story than dialogue. Narration is the author speaking to the reader. Through the use of narration, the author can tell the reader things no one else could possibly know. The author becomes all-knowing and can provide some of the most important details of the story.

A general rule to follow as you are writing narration is that it should flow from general to specific. Each topic should be introduced in general terms and then developed with explicit example. For instance, you might begin a paragraph describing a typical New England summer. That is your general statement and would be followed by details of what constitutes a typical New England summer.

Somewhere between dialogue and narration is "indirect discourse." This is a technique to keep a long speech from becoming a boring narration. In it, the author summarizes the speech with comment and description, using the actual words only to give color and flavor. Sometimes the speech is paraphrased, using direct quotes only for emphasis.

Dialogue, Not Conversation

People don't actually speak in dialogue, they speak in conversation. However, conversation, which includes pauses and stutters, is not suited for fiction. The dialogue of fiction must give the illusion of speech while being totally controlled by the author. Above all, dialogue must seem real.

Before attempting to write dialogue you must become familiar with human speech. Station yourself in some public place (a bus station, restaurant, or park bench) and listen to the way people talk.

Listen to the give and take. Listen to the rhythm. You'll more than likely hear conversation occurring in very short sentences. Some sentences will be little more than one word, maybe even a grunt. If you were to tape record a real conversation, you would find people clutter their speech with unnecessary fillers like "um," "uh," "er," and "ya know." These are conversational but definitely do not belong in dialogue, regardless of how real you want to make it sound.

A good way to learn dialogue writing techniques is to study some theatrical plays. Read them aloud and listen for the timing. Theatrical dialogue from modern plays shows us the essence of good dialogue. Writers of plays know what work the words must perform and they keep the story moving forward. In a play, as in your story, moments that aren't filled with dialogue are otherwise filled with action. The dialogue/action in a skillfully-written play will not come to a halt until the scene is finished.

In an effort to make dialogue seem real, some authors resort to using dialects. Every region of the United States has a unique dialect which is easy to understand for readers reared in that area, but which otherwise might as well be a different language altogether. Simply spelling words differently will not create dialect. Writing is meant to be read and understood. Using "thar" to mean their, "caw" to mean car, "dint" to mean didn't, or "Oil" to mean Earl will only succeed in confusing your reader. If the reader has to break concentration for even an instant and decipher what your characters are saying, you aren't doing a good job as a communicator. Mark Twain wrote Southern dialect with such skill that anyone could understand exactly what his characters were saying.

Once you decide upon using a dialect and you've researched it thoroughly, you must stick with it throughout the story. Characters who have grown up talking a certain way cannot change over the course of a story. To keep your characters from losing their dialect, write down key phrases in the Character Map and use them. But remember, don't overdo it.

Similar to dialect is lingo. Every occupation has its own associated way of talking. Doctors talk about "subdural hematomas," police officers call a car a "vehicle," and "You got yer ears on?" might be uttered by a truck driver. Elements of lingo can add flavor to your dialogue but, as with dialect, the meaning must be clear. In order for you to learn how doctors talk, you must listen to them. Don't assume what you hear on television or at the movies is an accurate representation. Television and movies can get away with using character cliches because this adds humor. Fiction filled with character cliches becomes artless.

In making your dialogue appear real, another area to watch out for is polysyllabism, the use of words containing many syllables. The majority of people talk using short, monosyllabic words in short, uncomplicated sentences. Unless your character is a college professor, keep the long, complex words to a minimum.

In real conversations, people rarely let other people talk for very long. Unless one character is lecturing another, lengthy speeches seem unnatural and tend to slow the pace. Keep your dialogue flowing by changing speakers frequently.

Once you have written dialogue, test your mastery by playing out the scene. Choose a partner (spouse or close friend) and read your dialogue aloud. Better yet, record it so you can play it back and analyze it afterwards. Does it sound real or is it stiff and artificial? Are the words you used words that a normal person would use in everyday speech? Does it flow in a logical progression? And, most important, does your dialogue make a point? Be critical. Nothing gives away an inexperienced writer as quickly as poor dialogue.

Sample Dialogue

As stated previously, the best way to learn how to write dialogue is to go out and start listening to the way people actually talk. Aside from that, the following examples of dialogue will illustrate some of the common faults and how they might be corrected.

> "You know, I'm pregnant," Angie said.
> "You're what?" Betty replied.
> "Pregnant. I found out this morning."
> "Whose is it?"

"Johnny's."

"How could you let ..."

"It was that weekend in Nassau. The sun, the sand. It really got to us."

"What are you going to do about it?"

"What can I do?"

"An abortion would be out of the question."

"Johnny would never go for that. What about marriage?"

"I really don't think marriage is in his plans."

The most obvious problem with the above is that, by the end, you aren't certain who is speaking. You could end every sentence with either "Betty said," or "Angie said," but that would become excruciatingly repetitive. A workable solution to this problem is to use narrative to help identify who is speaking. For instance:

"You know, I'm pregnant," Angie said.

"You're what?" Betty said, letting the dish she held slip from her hand and splash in the sink.

"Pregnant." Angie rubbed her hand over her developing stomach. "I found out this morning."

"Whose is it?" Betty said, trying to hide her disbelief by directing her attention to mopping up the water that had splashed from the sink.

"Johnny's." Angie twirled her hair nervously.

"How could you let ..."

"It was that weekend in Nassau," Angie began. "The sun, the sand. It really got to us."

"What are you going to do about it?"

"What can I do?"

"An abortion would be out of the question," Betty said, sitting down beside her friend.

"Johnny would never go for that. What about marriage?"

"Angie, I really don't think marriage is in his plans."

The second example makes it clear in the reader's mind who is speaking and also ties the dialogue to action, making the scene more interesting.   Not only can you make narrative references to your characters, but you can also have one character call the other by name. All this works to make your reader's job easier.

In an effort to avoid the repetition of "he said," and "she said," some authors will turn their dialogue into something totally artificial:

"So, are you going to take the job in Dubuque?" Roxanne queried.

Bramer hesitated, touching his chin and looking past Roxanne. "It is an excellent opportunity," he postulated.

"But you know I can't leave my career to follow you," Roxanne exclaimed.

"You must," Bramer pleaded. "I can't live without you."

"You'll have to choose," she threatened, "either your job or me."

There is nothing wrong with using "said" to identify your speakers. Words like "queried," "postulated," and "explained" often do more to detract from your dialogue than to help it. If your dialogue is interesting enough, your readers won't mind the repetition of "said."

In addition to substituting other verbs for "said," some authors include redundant adverbs, as in the following example:

"That was a fine supper," Abe said thankfully, lighting a cigar and drawing a long puff.

Millie looked away. "It's real easy cooking for a man like you," she said sheepishly.

"A man like me," he said inquiringly.

"A man I like," Millie said frankly.

These adverbs are unnecessary because they restate what the reader understands from the situation. If your character is giving a compliment, his appreciation is understood. If your character is acting sheepishly, you don't need to tell your reader she is talking sheepishly, also. Any time a character is asking a question, he is inquiring. Your dialogue should be written so that you don't have to qualify "said."

The next example, dialogue between two wranglers on a cattle drive, illustrates what happens when you let your characters slip out of character.

> "Cookie, dish me up another helpin' of them beans," Macon said, clanking his metal plate on the fire pit.
>
> "Rustled up some good chow tonight, ay?" Cookie prided himself on his ability to satisfy a cowhand's appetite.
>
> "Naw," said Macon, "after that trail dust I been eatin' all day, boot hide would taste jes as good."
>
> "Shucks, I was plannin' ta serve boot hide tomorrow," Cookie said, passing the plate back across the fire.
>
> "Cookie, your jocularity is paralleled only by your culinary expertise."

Clearly, no self-respecting cowboy would have said the final line of the preceding dialogue. Although this example is blatant, it does show the importance of knowing your characters and making certain that what they say in your story is what they would say in real life.

Some authors, knowing the importance of dialogue, will try to force their exposition into their characters speech. Any time you start dialogue with "as you may know," or have one character describe a present location to another character, you are undoubtedly misusing dialogue. The following example will illustrate.

> "Emily, just look at those mountains," Wendell said.
>
> "As you may know, Wendell, this is the largest mountain range in all of North America. It has jagged, snow-covered peaks which seem to reach higher than the clouds."
>
> "And," Wendell interrupted, "from the timberline down stands a dense, evergreen forest."

Obviously, the description of the mountain belongs in the narrative, rather than in dialogue.

"Emily, just look at those mountain," Wendell said.

The two beheld the largest mountain range in North America. A dense, evergreen forest stood below the timberline. Still higher, snow-covered peaks reached beyond the clouds.

Never use dialogue when narration would better accomplish your purpose.

Finally, the importance of using your Character Map can't be overemphasized when it comes to writing dialogue. Every character, in fiction and in real life, has a few key phrases which he will use repeatedly. A key phrase may consist of one or two unusual words which are unique to a character. These phrases distinguish one character from another and help your readers keep the players straight. For this reason, it is important to include key phrases and speech patterns in your Character Map and use them consistently from the beginning of your story to the end.

Writing Exercises

While attending a family gathering, or other similar situation of your choice, listen to a conversation in which you are not a speaker. As you listen, analyze what is being said. Try to pick out the purpose of this conversation. When you return to your writing area, turn the conversation you heard into tight (only the essential conversation with no "uh's" or "um's") dialogue. After you complete this, go back and trim out any lines which do not advance the dialogue's purpose.

Write two pages of dialogue depicting interaction between two characters: a man who has just come home from being fired from his job, and his wife who, unbeknownst to her husband, has just cleaned out the couple's savings account to purchase a new dining room set. Make sure your dialogue helps develop the characters, involves action, and conveys information. Because this should be an emotion-filled scene, use as little narration as necessary.

Alternately, write a scene as outlined above using two characters and a situation of your choosing.

Write a two-page scene, combining dialogue and narration, in which your main character is lost in the woods with only his faithful dog at his side. In this case, your character will be talking to himself and to his dog. Naturally, the dog will not answer, but as is common with the owners of pets, your character may answer for the animal.

7

Thematics

Now that you have considered plot, characters, and how characters talk, it's time to move on to what gives literature its monumental
importance: theme.

The theme of a story does not start or end on the written page. In
fact, it may never even appear in written form in your story. You, as
the author, may not even be aware of its presence.

Theme is neither character or plot, though both of these figure
prominently into it. The theme of a story actually embodies the entire
story, cover to cover, reducing all of the author's words to a basic
human truth. The mechanics of this interplay of character, plot, and
theme is termed thematics.

A Job For The Critics

The abstract concept of "theme" is often addressed by literature
teachers, analyzed by critics, and pondered by students. Yet, when
asked about the meaning of a work of fiction, most authors will talk
about the characters, the locations, and the action. They often say they
don't know what the story means or that it means whatever the reader
wants it to mean. To further complicate the issue, the meaning can
change over time.

It is the literary critics who, after analyzing a work of fiction, often assign meaning to a story. Students, teachers, and other critics are really the only readers who are interested in having the meaning of fiction explained. For most sophisticated readers, a critical review which sets a theme to a story is like having a food critic explain what a particular gourmet dish tastes like. Food, like fiction, must be savored by the individual. The critic has no better idea of the true meaning than the average reader and, if the meaning is so unclear that it has to be interpreted, the writer has done a poor job of communicating.

Just as no one can teach you how to write fiction, no one can tell you how to give significance to your works of fiction. Significance is something a story either has or doesn't have. You must, however, be aware that such significance does exist.

The Meaning Of Fiction

Simply stated, the "theme" is the meaning of fiction: what your story will be remembered for. The theme is not something you can impose on your story, but must be brought forth from the story. Furthermore, the theme must not be confused with the moral or plot, as it is not the lesson taught or the sequence of the action.

Rarely does an author come out and identify the theme directly. Rather, the theme is implied.

To begin a discussion of fictional themes, you must first realize there exist several levels at which fiction is consumed. The most superficial level of reading is for pure entertainment. At this level, a reader may read for characterization, meeting different characters as one would meet new friends and becoming immersed in their problems. He may read for the suspense or anxiety produced by an intriguing plot. He may read stories set in exotic locations out of curiosity. Or he may read because he admires a particular writer's style. This type of reader will read whether or not the story presents an important theme.

At more profound levels, the reader seeks a comment on human values and conduct. These readers are concerned with good and bad, truth and dishonesty, and what place humans occupy in the world.

Humans generally have a basic need to put things in order. A writer creates an imaginary world of characters and events, and the thematic structure puts order to these story elements. By the end of the story, these readers expect to be different: they expect a growth experience. Without a recognizable theme your writing will lack significance in the minds of these readers and they will look elsewhere for intellectual satisfaction.

The nature of the story does not prevent it from being a thematic work. Even comedies can have a theme. By itself, comedy implies a view of life. In fiction, comedic themes use comedy, the contrast of disappointment, and surprise.

In comedy or in drama, an author can't start a writing project by picking a theme and writing his story to that theme. The theme comes from the deepest recesses of the author's mind. Often, the author doesn't even sense a theme when he puts pen to paper. The very reason some authors write is because a deeply moving experience has changed them and they feel compelled to communicate their personal experiences and beliefs. So the author relates a story, hoping to change the reader as he has been changed.

The theme takes shape from the interplay of the characters and is illustrated through the plot. Keep in mind that the theme is an abstraction and must not be confused with the plot. The plot may not apply to all readers, but the theme must apply to the greatest number of people as possible. By definition, in fact, it must apply to all of mankind.

For example, a story of two young, star-crossed lovers who are kept apart by their feuding families only to end up killing themselves may not seem relevant to every reader. The reader may never have been involved in a like situation, nor may he ever expect to be. Yet, the theme of this story, that all human events seem trivial when measured against the finality of death, can be understood by everyone because it is a universal truth of human nature. To illustrate: William Shakespeare penned "Romeo and Juliet" in the late 1500's and, though the story is anything but modern, the theme is as relevant today as when it was first played out on stage.

The theme is different from the topic of your story and is not

necessarily proportional to it. The story's topic could be love, growing up, or war. The theme is the comment on the topic that is implied
by the story. Even if the subject of your story is seemingly insignificant, the theme must be grand.

It is important not to confuse theme with information. In Herman
Melville's epic novel, ''Moby-Dick,'' the author provides page after
page of information about whaling, yet whaling is not the theme of the
story. The theme of this story, as generally accepted by critics, is,
''Man's ability to conquer nature fails except in his ability to conquer
is own human nature.'' Of course, no two people will interpret a story
in exactly the same way. A reader's interpretation is based on his
personal experiences and beliefs.

Development Of Theme In Literature

The concept of theme is nothing new. Since the beginning of
storytelling, when stories were passed from one generation to the next
as a way of teaching human values, themes have figured prominently.

Children's stories, in general, and the Bible, in particular, use
examples of the most simple thematic methods: allegories, parables,
and fables. An allegory is a presentation of an idea in simple narrative
where the events and characters are understood to be direct equivalents
to elements involved in the statement of the human truth. Parables and
fables are short allegories with a single definite moral. Fables make
use of inanimate objects or animals which act and speak as humans for
the purpose of moral instruction. (Remember that the theme suggests
morality but does not offer a moral.)

Through the ages, stories have become more complex and critics
have delved ever deeper to discover, or create, the hidden meaning of
fiction.

To further distinguish theme from other elements of a story,
consider Rudyard Kipling's ''The Man Who Would Be King.'' This
is the story of a man who happens into and out of a leadership position.
The topic might be ''India,'' as that is where this story is set. The

moral of this story, the lesson that it teaches, is, "Don't try to be something you aren't." And the theme, as it is most generally agreed, is, "True kingship is found in the exercise of power over one's self."

The theme of John Keats's poem, "Ode on a Grecian Urn," might be, "The shortness of human life is insignificant when compared to the permanence of art."

One theme that has been exploited over time, turning up frequently in lyric poetry, is "carpe diem," a Latin phrase which means "seize the day." Here, the human truth to be passed on is that youth is fleeting and pleasure should be pursued vigorously.

Other memorable themes from literature include:

Human virtue is to be found in the most unlikely places and under the most unlikely conditions.

The fact of death breaks through all of man's attempts to rationalize it.

Man must come to terms with the discovery of the nature of evil.

The bottom line for the author is this: whether you recognize it at the outset, your work of fiction must have a point which your readers will accept as being important. If the majority of readers reach the end of your story and ask, "What's the point?", you haven't done your job as a storyteller. The key to insuring a "point" to your story is to begin with passion for the story you seek to tell. If you write to write, your story will be shallow. If you write from passion, your story will have significance.

Writing Exercises

Although you will probably never write a story to a theme, this exercise is intended to help you recognize the elements of thematic development. To begin, conceive five themes which embody a basic human truth and write them in sentence form as shown earlier in this chapter. From these five, choose one and write a two-page plot outline to show how you would illustrate this theme. The plot does not have to be complicated, but you must include all the plot elements discussed in Chapter 5.

8

Style and Revision

If you have chosen to make writing your career, words will become your way of life. Words are a writer's most important and most versatile tool. Letters go together to form syllables, syllables combine to make words, words are strung together to compose sentences, and sentences are woven into paragraphs. Most every word has a precise meaning and can be blended with other words to convey literally any thought, any feeling, even any sensation.

The professional writer is expected to be an expert on words and how they are assembled, including such basic areas as spelling, vocabulary, punctuation, grammar, sentence structure, and composition. These constitute ''style'' and, for most, are the skills we spent the first seventeen years of our lives trying to avoid. The utter complexity of the English language makes its mastery difficult. Fully eighty-percent of the American population has deficient communication skills. Only a fraction of a percent of the remaining populace would be qualified to teach English, even at the grade school level.

There are famous writers today who are admittedly poor spellers or grammarians. Fortunately, they can afford to hire secretaries to correct their flawed manuscripts.

For the beginning writer, who doesn't have the luxury of having someone else polish his prose, style is preeminently important. Style errors are an indication of an inexperienced writer and will keep your manuscript from getting past even the mailroom editor.

Closely associated with style, insofar as it deals with the mechanics of writing, is revision. Through cutting, editing, tightening, and general reworking, revision can take an average work of fiction and turn it into a best-seller.

This chapter will reacquaint the writer with the basic elements of style and provide a basis for becoming your own editor. Even if you think you know all there is to know about style, this section will provide a valuable review and a useful reference for the future.

Tools Of The Wordsmith

Some of the most basic tools a writer has at his disposal are dictionaries, thesauruses, and style manuals.

The following is a list of books which every writer should have close at hand. You will find that a small investment in reference books will provide enormous returns which pay off year after year.

The Merriam-Webster Dictionary - pocket edition. This paperback boasts, ''more definitions than any other pocket dictionary.'' It is the reference you will use more than any other. Expect to replace this book every five years due to wear.

Webster's New Twentieth Century Dictionary - unabridged. Although the paperback dictionary will ordinarily be your first choice for checking spelling and definitions, an unabridged dictionary provides greater depth. These dictionaries can be quite expensive, but past editions are often discounted significantly by many bookstores.

Roget's Thesaurus in Dictionary Form. The purpose of a thesaurus is to give the writer a variety of words to choose from. It is a legitimate tool and can help you find the exact word to say what you want to say. Alphabetical tabs will help speed your search.

New Rhyming Dictionary and Poets' Handbook. Although this book is aimed at poets, it can be just as useful to the writer of prose. Like the thesaurus, this book is filled with words which are grouped according to their endings and number of syllables. It can be helpful when you are looking for just the right word.

The New York Times Manual of Style and Usage. This is the essential reference for reporters at the New York Times and most other English-written newspapers around the world. Its purpose is to provide standards for journalists and includes specifics on word use, capitalization, punctuation, abbreviations, and much more.

A Manual for Writers of Term Paper, Theses, and Dissertations by Kate L. Turabian. Although the title sounds pretty lofty, this book contains a wealth of information concerning style. It sets standards for spelling, capitalization, punctuation, quotations, numbers, and abbreviations. The book's format makes it quite easy to use.

Strunk and White's The Elements of Style. A handy reference in thin, paperback form. It's been required reading in high school composition classes since its first publishing in 1935, and includes rules for using commas, principles of composition, and a list of words and expressions which are commonly misused.

Bartlett's Familiar Quotations. This reference contains quotes from famous literary works, from the Bible and Shakespeare, through presidential speeches. It shows you how other writers have put words together in a way that was deemed important enough to be remembered. It is intended to serve the fiction writer as a source for inspiration, rather than a source for words.

The Macmillan Handbook of English by John M. Kierzek and Walker Gibson - Any English text book will round out your reference library.

This is by no means a comprehensive list. You may be able to get along with less, or you may need more. The more references you have, the less likely you'll be to get bogged down when trying to find just the right word or searching for the proper way to use punctuation. These books may overlap in content, but they are useful in that they provide different perspectives on the same topics.

The Parts Of Speech

Although the following definitions may seem unnecessarily simple, these elements of speech will be referred to repeatedly and are worth having grouped together for quick reference.

Noun - A word that names something. As taught in school, a noun is a person, place, or thing.

Verb - An action word.

Pronoun - A word that takes the place of a noun. There are five classes of pronouns: personal pronouns (I, you, he, she, it, they, we, them, thee, thou), demonstrative pronouns (this, that, these, those), relative pronouns (who, which, what, that, whoever, whatever, whichever), interrogative pronouns (who, which, what), and indefinite pronouns (one, some, none, any, anyone, anybody, someone, each, somebody, nobody, everyone, everybody, either, neither, both).

Adjective - A word that describes or limits a noun or pronoun, usually denoting quality, quantity, or extent.

Adverb - A word that modifies a verb, an adjective, or another adverb.

Preposition - A word used to show a relationship between a noun or pronoun, called the object of the preposition, and another word in a sentence.

Conjunction - A word which connects words, phrases, or clauses, such as and, but, yet, and nor.

Interjection - A word or group of words used as an exclamation to express sudden or strong feelings.

Verbals - These are words which are derived from verbs, have some of the forms and functions of verbs, but are used primarily as other parts of speech. They include gerunds (a verbal used as a noun), participles (a verbal used as an adjective), and infinitives (a verbal used as a noun, an adjective, or an adverb, and ordinarily preceded by the word, ''to'').

Sentence - The basic unit of language, made up of at least one independent finite verb with its subject.

Paragraph - A unit of communication in which one or more sentences which deal with the same topic or the words of one speaker are combined.

COMMON STYLE ERRORS
Spelling

Spelling is one of the most annoying errors for editors and one of the easiest to correct. Some editors will refuse to read a manuscript fraught by many misspelled words. Your personal policy should be: when in doubt about the spelling of a word, look it up. That's why you have a dictionary and editors expect you to be able to use it.

Word processing programs which feature a spelling checker are useful, but don't rely on them too heavily. They are only as good as the words which are programmed into them. Typically, you won't find proper names or geographic locations in even the best spell checking system, nor will you find every verb tense.

The following list of rules will help eliminate some of the most common spelling errors.

1. Before adding a suffix to a word ending in a silent "e", you generally drop the "e" before a suffix beginning with a vowel (believe + able = believable), but retain the "e" before a suffix beginning with a consonant (force + ful = forceful). If the "e" follows a "c" or "g" and the suffix begins with an "a" or "o", retain the "e" to indicate the soft sound of the "c" or "g" (courage + ous = courageous).

2. In words containing "ie" or "ei", if the sound is a long "e", "i" comes before "e" except after "c" (achieve, receipt).

3. In one-syllable words, and words accented on the last syllable, which end in a single consonant, preceded by a single vowel, the final consonant is doubled before adding a suffix which begins with a vowel (cut + ing = cutting, admit + ing = admitting).

Grammar

Although not as easy to correct as spelling, grammatical errors are no less glaring to an editor.

The following are some of the most common grammatical errors and how they can be fixed.

1. Misdirected Modifiers - Misdirected modifiers are phrases, clauses, or words which either do not refer to the subject of the sentence or are not logically placed next to the word they modify.

Incorrect: Having an injured wing, flight was impossible.
(The author does not indicate what had an injured wing.)
Correct: Having an injured wing, it was impossible for the bird to fly.
Incorrect: Running through the neighborhood, the apartments seemed vacant and foreboding. (Were the apartments running?)
Correct: As I ran through the neighborhood, the apartments seemed vacant and foreboding.

2. Subject/Verb Agreement - A single subject must have a singular verb, while a plural subject must have a plural verb. In a simple sentence, this is easy to see. You would never say, "The boys is running." However, when the subject is separated from the verb or the sentence structure is unusual, the author may forget the subject of the sentence.

Incorrect: The commotion made by all of those children were nerve-racking. (The subject is "commotion," not "children," so the verb must be singular.)
Correct: The commotion made by all of those children was nerve-racking.
Incorrect: None of the miners were injured as a result of the cave-in. ("None" means "not one" and always takes a single verb.)
Correct: None of the miners was injured as a result of the cave-in.

3. Pronoun Agreement - The pronoun must agree in number, person, and gender with the noun or pronoun to which it refers.

Incorrect: Each member of the team had their own uniform.
("Each" is singular, "their" is plural.)
Correct: Each member of the team had his own uniform.

4. Reflexive Pronouns - The reflexive pronoun (ending in "-self" or "-selves") must refer to the subject of the sentence when the subject also receives the action in the sentence.

Incorrect: The judge awarded damages from the accident to Mr. Johnson and myself.
Correct: The judge awarded damages from the accident to Mr. Johnson and me.
Incorrect: Mr. Johnson, the attorney, and myself left the courtroom after the trial.
Correct: Mr. Johnson, Mrs. Elliot, and I left the courtroom after the trial.

5. Parallel Construction - One technique for making writing easier to understand is parallel construction. Through its use, the writer gives elements that are equal in a sentence the same grammatical form.

Not Parallel: A writer should be dedicated, have ample talent, and possess ambition.
Parallel: A writer should be dedicated, talented, and ambitious.

6. Sentence Fragments - A sentence fragment is an incomplete sentence lacking a subject, a verb, or both. There are times in fiction writing when a sentence fragment can be used effectively to communicate a point, as when used for emphasis. People frequently speak in sentence fragments, so dialogue is often full of them. However, the mistaken use, or the overuse, of sentence fragments makes writing choppy and often unclear.

Fragmented: Adrianne was a beautiful woman. And a nice
  dresser, too. (The second phrase is the fragment.)
Un-fragmented: Adrianne was a beautiful woman and a nice
  dresser.

7. Run-on Sentences - A run-on sentence is created when the writer links two or more complete sentences without proper punctuation between them.

Incorrect: The sunset was extraordinary, she could not see it for
  the trees.
Correct: The sunset was extraordinary, but she could not see it
  for the trees.

8. Passive Voice - Although not necessarily a mistake, the passive voice is less direct than the active voice. The active voice puts the subject first, followed by the verb and the object, whereas the passive voice turns things around, putting the object at the beginning of the sentence and the subject at the end. Various forms of the verb "to be" often indicate the passive voice.

Passive: The flat tire was fixed by Ralph.
Active: Ralph fixed the flat tire.

Punctuation

Speech is not a continuous, monotonal delivery of words. There are pauses, certain words are stressed, and the pitch and speed of delivery change to reflect excitement. When we speak, each thought is nicely packaged with emphasis at the beginning and a pause to signal the end. We exclaim and we question.

In writing, the inflection of our voice is absent, so we must use some technique to help our reader understand the human emotion which lies within our prose. To accomplish this, we use punctuation.

Without any punctuation, writing would be impossible to understand. Since our goal is communication, it is important to use accepted standards, such as the following examples.

1. Question Mark - Use a question mark to denote direct questions (these usually have the subject preceded by the verb and begin with "who," "what," "when," etc.). Do not use a question mark at the end of an indirect question.

Direct: What does she think about me?
Indirect: I wonder what she thinks about me.

2. Exclamation Point - Just as with the boy who cried wolf, the exclamation point should be used sparingly, and only after a statement that is truly exclamatory. Its overuse can dilute its meaning.

Correct: Help!
Incorrect: I think I may need help!

3. Comma - A comma can perform three types of functions. It can (1) link independent clauses which are joined by a coordinating conjunction (and, but, or, nor, for, so, yet), (2) enclose parenthetical information, simple definitions, or interrupting expressions in a sentence, and (3) separate introductory clauses or phrases from the rest of the sentence.

Link: Milo wanted to continue the conversation, but Emma
       would have nothing to do with him.
Enclose: Milo Bail, the most handsome player on the varsity
          basketball team, would have done anything to win the
          attention of Emma Lou.
Separate: Playing basketball takes coordination, height, and
           endurance. (The final comma is for clarity.)
Separate: The gymnasium was dedicated in Tacoma,
           Washington, on November 23, 1988, as part of
           National Fitness Week.

4. Quotation Marks - Quotation marks are used in fiction to show

4. Quotation Marks - Quotation marks are used in fiction to show that a character is speaking. The most frequent mistakes in using quotation marks are in using them with other punctuation.

> Correct: "Is that Mary Rogers?" the man asked.
> Correct: "That is Mary Rogers," the man said.
> Correct: "Oh no!" Mary screamed. "That can't be my
>   brother."

5. Semicolon - The semicolon marks a greater break in the continuity of a sentence than is indicated by a comma. Use a semicolon between parts of a compound sentence when they are not connected by a conjunction, or for emphasis when a conjunction is present.

> Correct: The judge sat down; the jury remained standing.
> Correct: The judge sat down; however, the jury remained
>   standing.

6. Colon - The colon indicates a discontinuity of construction which is greater than that indicated by a semicolon. The colon is used to introduce a clause or phrase that expands, clarifies, or exemplifies what precedes it.

> Correct: She was a classic beauty: tall, slender, and graceful.

Vocabulary

The English language contains well over one million words, of which forty percent belong to specialized fields (e.g., medicine, engineering, law, etc.). Those words which remain for the author's use provide both benefit and vexation. With so many words to choose from, selecting just one is often difficult. It is the author's job to use the words which communicate his thoughts the best. The better one's vocabulary, the easier this job will be.

There is no easy way to develop a powerful vocabulary. Those

ing and listening to educated people speak. As a writer, it is important that you read constantly. This not only improves your vocabulary, but also trains your mind to think in sentences and paragraphs. Another technique for building word power is reading the dictionary.

As beneficial as a good vocabulary can be, keep in mind that your readers may not be as well-read as you are. You should always use the best word, but don't go out of your way to use obscure words. These will be distracting for your reader.

It's interesting to note that most mistakes in vocabulary are the result of simple words being used incorrectly. Homonyms, words which sound alike but have very different meanings, can be a source of much confusion.

The following is a list of words which are misused most frequently.

Affect / Effect - Affect is a verb and means to influence, change, or to have an effect on something. It can also mean to wear or use, or to pretend (as in an affectation). Effect means to accomplish, complete, make possible, or carry out. Almost always, in the case of a noun, effect is the correct word (e.g., One effect of nuclear disarmament is world peace.).

Allusion / Illusion - Allusion means to refer to something indirectly. An illusion is a misconception.

Capital / Capitol - The capital is the city where state and federal governments conduct business. The Capitol is a specific national or state building.

Everyone / Every One - Everyone means the entire group. Every one means each one.

Flaunt/Flout - To flaunt is to make a impudent display, while flout means to make a mockery of something or someone.

Hanged / Hung - A person is hanged, a picture is hung.

Immigrate / Emigrate - Immigrate refers to going into a country, while emigrate refers to leaving a country.

Imply / Infer - The speaker implies by implanting allusions, while the listener infers what is said and makes his own conclusions.

Lay / Lie - Lay means to put or to place and requires a direct object. Lie means to be in a reclining position and does not require a direct object.

Principal / Principle - Principal is used as a noun to mean the chief person, or as an adjective to mean first in importance. A principle is a fundamental truth.

Simile / Metaphor - A simile makes a direct and explicit comparison of two dissimilar things and is usually introduced by like, as, or as if. A metaphor implies a comparison through the substitution of one word or idea for another. Simile - The boat is like a steel plow. Metaphor - The boat plows through the water.

Who / Whom - Use who to mean he, she, or they. Use whom to mean him, her, or them.

COMPOSITION

Composition, by definition, is the arranging of elements in an artistic form. The elements available to the writer for arranging are words. Words are strung together into sentences; sentences go together to form paragraphs.

The artistry comes from the writer's ability to make the words, the sentences, and the paragraphs interesting, while flowing smoothly from one to another.

Sentence Structure

One method for making prose more readable is varying sentence length and structure. Although there is no formula to follow, good writing should consist of short sentences mixed with long sentences, and simple sentences combined with compound and complex sentences.

A simple sentence is one that contains a single independent clause, with or without modifiers. An independent clause can stand alone as a sentence, while a subordinate, or dependent, clause depends on some other element within a sentence, functioning as a noun, adjective, or adverb. A simple sentence may contain compounded subjects, verbs, or both.

Simple: Women and men work and sleep.

Compound sentences are made by joining two or more sentences using conjunctions and proper punctuation.

Compound: Women work, while men work and play.

Notice that in the above example, the comma plays an important part in how the sentence will be read. Without the comma, the sentence means that women are working during the same time as men are working and playing.

A complex sentence has at least one main clause that is capable of standing alone, and one or more dependent clauses which are joined to the main clause by a relative pronoun (who, which, that) or a subordinating conjunction (after, although, as, because, before, if, since, when, where, why).

Complex: Her argument, that women work harder than men, was based solely on her personal opinion.

As you write, you will not necessarily be able to consciously vary your sentence structure. However, as you begin editing and revising your manuscript, take note of composition. If all your sentences seem to be short, or all connected by ''and'' or ''but,'' work at adding some variety.

Paragraphs

A paragraph is a sentence, or a group of sentences, which deal with a single topic or the words of a single speaker. A good paragraph must have unity, order, and development.

Unity means that a paragraph focuses on a single, clear idea and that all the sentences of the paragraph deal with that idea. The central idea is often expressed in the first or last sentence of the paragraph, and is called the topic sentence.

For a paragraph to have order, the sentences must be arranged in

For a paragraph to have order, the sentences must be arranged in a logical progression and must flow easily from one to another. Frequently in fiction, the orderly flow is from general to specific. The topic sentence introduces the general idea of the paragraph, and all the other sentences give specific details to support the idea.

Development requires that enough details and examples be presented to make the central idea clear to the reader. Some methods of development include chronological, comparison and contrast, cause and effect, and classification.

Paragraphs aren't intended to stand alone, so the end of one paragraph must lead naturally into the beginning of the next.

Just as sentence length should vary for interest, the length of paragraphs should vary, also. A page containing a single long paragraph is intimidating, while a page with a mixture of short and longer paragraphs is more inviting. If you notice your paragraphs running long, trim out words or split the paragraph into two. On the other hand, if your manuscript is filled with page after page of single-sentence paragraphs, your prose may lack development and need more examples.

REVISION

There are basically three levels of revision your manuscript will face between the time when you first put words to paper and the time when your book is published or your play performed. These are (1) the revisions you make as you are writing, (2) the revisions you make after the first draft of your manuscript is complete, and (3) the revisions an editor will make prior to publication. Upon each of these levels may be many other steps. Some authors revise a book manuscript five times before they're satisfied. It's not unusual for a book to be reviewed by three or more editors before it is set in type for publication. Each level presents opportunities for you to improve the quality of your writing.

Periodically as you are writing, you should pause and read what you have written. Sometimes a writer will get so caught up in the act of writing that the logical progression of the story will suffer. This is to revise your first draft. This revision takes place at the word, sentence, and paragraph levels. Check carefully for style errors. Are words spelled correctly? Do the sentences follow accepted rules of grammar? Have you selected the best word for what you are trying to communicate? Do your paragraphs have a topic sentence? Do the paragraphs completely develop the central idea?

A good time to make revision is before you begin writing for the day. Take a few minutes and review what you wrote the day before. This not only gives you an opportunity to make changes, it also brings you up to speed as far as where your story was when you stopped the day before.

The second revision takes place at the story level and is the most important. Here, you have to look at your story as a reader would. In order for you to transform yourself from writer to reader, it's best to let your manuscript sit in a drawer for a week. Then, with pencil in hand, read the story and imagine it was written by someone else. Make notes in the margins and keep an eye out for typographical and style errors you may have missed the first time through.

Keep an eye out for awkward transitions between scenes and scenes that last too long. Many writers, especially new authors, will get so enthralled with describing a setting, character, or situation that the pacing of the story will come to a screeching halt. The pace of your story is of prime importance, and anything that slows the pace, no matter how good you think it is, must be eliminated. If, after reading a particularly long description, you can't easily remember what went on immediately before, the description is too detailed.

The process of tightening your prose is something you have to practice. Most people communicate with too many words. By removing all words that do not directly advance the story, your writing will become sharper and easier to read and understand. You have to be your own harshest critic when it comes to revision. Obviously, you thought all the words you put down on the paper were important to the story, or else you wouldn't have written them. Now you must ask yourself if your reader's understanding of the story would suffer by the elimination of words. It is not uncommon for even best-selling authors to edit out ten to twenty percent of the words in a manuscript before submitting it for publication.

The form your final draft takes is important for the editors, who estimate word counts based on the number of pages submitted, and for the typesetters, who take your manuscript and set it into book page format.

For your manuscript, use 8 1/2- by 11-inch white typing paper of a good quality. Don't use erasable bond or onion skin, as these allow the type to be easily smeared. Put a new ribbon in your typewriter or computer printer, and make sure the letters print clearly. Only use computer printers that are capable of near letter quality type or better, as the others make reading difficult for an editor. The margins on each edge should be 1 1/4 inches and your last name and the page number should appear in the upper right hand corner of each page. Manuscripts should not be bound. Submit them in a cardboard stationery box. Short manuscripts should be paper clipped together. Make sure that you keep a copy of any manuscript you submit. Manuscripts do get lost in the mail and often get misplaced in a publisher's mailroom. (More information on manuscript submission appears in the following chapter.)

The final revision of your manuscript is handled by the editor, an employee of the publisher. Some publishers have two or three levels of editors who perform separate functions. Junior editors will sort out manuscripts which they believe have enough potential for a senior editor to read. Together, these two editors will determine whether your story fits into the plans of the publisher. The story editor will check your story for correctness of facts, for erroneous shifts in time and location, and for other details.

If major revisions are deemed necessary, the editor will return the manuscript to you with suggestions for rewriting. Few manuscripts go directly from writer to printer without some amount of revision from the editor.

When your manuscript comes back from the editor, or when you receive the galleys (long sheets of type which are ready to be assembled into pages of a book), it is likely you'll see hand-written proofreader's marks throughout the text and in the margins. These marks tell the typesetter what changes need to be made. The most commonly used proofreader's marks are shown on page 116. The galleys represent your last chance to find errors before your book goes to press, so it's important that you examine them closely and make clear notations of any errors you find.

By following accepted rules of style and grammar you can generate a professional-looking manuscript which editors will read. Correct style does not guarantee success, but its lack will certainly guarantee failure.

Writing Exercises

The importance of tightening a story to improve pacing can't be overstressed. To practice this, turn back to the writing exercises in Chapter 3 where you were asked to write a two page description. Take those two pages and edit out all the non-essential material so you are left with only the most important details. You should be able to cut out a minimum of fifty percent of the words.

Proofreader's Marks

Λ	Insert character	AWK	Awkward construction
⌒	Delete space, close up	lc- ¢	Change to lowercase
ℰ	Delete and close up	Caps	Change to capital
#	Insert space	S.C.	Set in small caps
eq #	Make space between words equal	ital	Set in italic
√√√	Correct letterspacing	rom	Set in roman
ℙ	Start paragraph	B.F.	Set in boldface
no ℙ	No paragraph, run together	w.f.	Wrong font
⊐	Move type one em from left to right	X	Reset broken character
]	Flush right	↺	Reverse, type upside down
[	Flush left	,/	Insert comma
][	Center	ᵛ	Insert apostrophe
[ ]	Justify	⌣⌣	Insert quotation marks
⊓	Move up	⊙	Insert period
⊔	Move down	|?|	Insert question mark
tr ∿	Transpose characters	;|	Insert semicolon
(SP)	Spell out word	:|	Insert colon
stet	Let it stand, don't change	|=|	Insert hyphen
		1/M	Insert em dash

9

The Business of Fiction Writing

Generally, authors are not very good business managers. A writer typically just wants to write, leaving the business concerns to someone else. This is the reason why there are literary agents. For the beginning writer, as well as for the seasoned professional, it's important to have a basic understanding of business matters in order for you not to be taken advantage of.

This chapter looks at the basics of business for the author.

Your Own Business

As stated at the beginning of this book, in order for you to succeed as a writer, you must approach writing as a business. You are in business for yourself. You must have enough drive to push yourself hard because no one else will. You control your future. Your success or failure is in your hands.

For any business to exist, it must have a physical location and a product to sell. In your case, the location will most likely be a corner of your home. Even though it's only a corner, it's important that you set it up as an office. Assemble the materials you will use in your business, including a desk and chair, reference books, a typewriter or word processor, paper, and pencils or pens. A telephone is not necessary, or even desirable, as it will serve only as a distraction.

The product you sell is words on paper. Before you can make a sale, you must first manufacture a product. This is why it is important that you write every day. Any day that you don't write, you lose your ability to generate sales. You could start with a single, novel-length product, or you could diversify and start with several shorter pieces. The greater the number of products you have, the better your chances are of making a sale.

Now that you have a business location and a product, the next step is advertising that product. Professional stationery isn't required, but it is a nice touch and does give your business a little credibility. Business cards are also good, and can be purchased for as little as $10 for 1,000 cards. Calling yourself a writer or author on a business card may be presumptuous, until you have actually made a sale. It would be better to list ''Literary Services'' under your name. This sounds a little more professional and may actually help an unsolicited manuscript get past the mailroom editor.

In addition to the personal benefits you'll realize from setting up an office, your tax advisor can help you realize financial benefits, as well. As a business, the Internal Revenue Service gives you three years in which to make your business profitable. If, after that time, you still haven't made any profit, the IRS considers that your business is really a hobby and will no longer allow deductions. If you haven't made any money at writing after three years, it's reasonable to expect that you should consider another business. In fact, within your first year as a writer, you should have completed at least one book-length manuscript and several other short projects, or you may not be taking writing as seriously as you should.

Query First

It is a standard practice in the writing business that, unless otherwise specified, your first contact with a publisher should be in the form of a query letter.

"Query" literally means "to question." In a query letter, the writer asks an editor whether he would be interested in reading a manuscript. Queries are also used by free-lance writers to solicit writing assignments.

More than a quarter of the book publishers in America will return an unsolicited manuscript to the author unread and usually unopened. There are two reasons for this. First, publishers feel they are not in the business of training authors. Even with a selling author, the publisher will have a large cash investment in time spent by editors, typesetters, proofreaders, artists, printers, and salespeople. The cost of having editors evaluate entire manuscripts from unpublished authors is simply too high. (To varying degrees, however, editors have been given the opportunity by their employers to develop promising new authors, so there is hope.)

Second, there is the question of liability. As soon as an editor opens an unsolicited manuscript he runs the risk of a rejected author claiming the theft of his story ideas. This is the very reason why television and movie producers deal exclusively through agents who are known to them.

If you know an editor wants to read a query before he sees the finished manuscript, you'll save yourself time and postage by complying.

The proper query letter should contain four parts: a resume of previous publications, the writer's particular qualifications which make him capable of writing the piece in question, a brief summation of the story, and permission to submit the finished manuscript.

A list of previous publications is hard to come by for a beginning writer. Instead of stating that you have never before been published, skip this. You'll have to rely on your letter-writing ability to prove your communication skills.

The second part of your letter sells you as the only one who could possibly tell your story. If an exotic location is important to your plot, let the editor know that you lived there all your life. If you have written a mystery and you're a police detective, let the editor know.

Next, tell what your story is about in the fewest possible words. Here, you don't want to tell how the story ends. Your goal is to give enough information to interest the editor and make him want to know more. This part of your letter is the most important. It's similar to the first paragraph of your story, where you hook the reader.

Finally, ask for permission to submit the story, or the first few chapters, to the editor personally.

It is important that your letter be brief and to the point, a maximum of two pages in length. Editors are busy people. They spend long hours pouring over manuscripts and will appreciate you getting straight to the point in your letter.

Some publishers include additional specifications as to how they prefer to be queried. They may ask to see your first three chapters, a chapter-by-chapter outline, or both. Some publishers will accept completed manuscripts. It is always best to follow the publisher's established policy when querying. It will save you time and make you appear more professional.

When sending a query letter to a publisher, addressing it to an editor by name will give you a better chance of your letter being read. Otherwise, just like mail addressed to "occupant", your letter may sit in a huge pile that will be sorted by a secretary when she runs out of other work. Names of editors can be found in the "LMP: Literary Market Place/ Directory of American Book Publishers" at your library.

If you don't receive a reply to your query within eight weeks, it is acceptable to telephone the editor and inquire as to the status of your proposal. You will most likely reach his assistant who will look for your material and call you back at a later time.

Manuscript Form

Just as there is a specific way to ask an editor to read your manuscript, there are also standards to follow when preparing your manuscript.

Your manuscripts should always be typed, double-spaced on good quality 8 1/2- by 11-inch white paper, using black ink. Erasable bond paper will smear, and thin papers won't last for more than one or two submissions.

Use only standard type faces. Don't use script type as this is exceptionally difficult to read. If you are using a computer printer, make sure the printing is letter quality. If you can see distinct dot patterns in the letters, the quality is not good enough. Also, before typing your finished draft, put a new ribbon in your typewriter.

Manuscript margins are important. You should have 1 1/4-inch margins on all sides of the page. These margins provide a place for an editor to write notes and typesetting directions. In addition, the editor can judge the length of the entire manuscript based on the number of pages if standard margins are observed.

The first page of a book manuscript is the title page. It should have your name and address in the upper left-hand corner, the title and by-line centered about halfway down the page, and the approximate word count 1/4 of the way up from the bottom. The first page of text should begin halfway down the page, as should the first page of successive chapters. Every page after the title page should bear your last name and the page number in the upper right-hand corner.

Book manuscripts should be submitted in a stationery box, un-bound. Manuscripts for short articles should be paper clipped together. Editors frequently take work home and a bound manuscript is bulky and hard to handle.

In manuscript presentation, neatness counts. Numerous strike overs and erasures will distract the reader. If you are not a competent typist, it will be worth the expense to have your manuscript typed professionally. Fees for typing are about $1 per page with spell checking provided at no additional charge. When you receive the completed manuscript, it's important to proofread it. Errors made by the typist should be corrected at no additional charge. You should expect to pay for errors which you made or any other changes.

Opinion varies considerably on the topic of photocopied submissions. A question an editor is bound to ask when he receives a photocopied manuscript is, "Has this manuscript been simultaneously submitted to other publishers?" Because a publisher invests time and expense in evaluating manuscripts, he is less likely to read a manuscript which is a simultaneous submission. Whether or not you submit your manuscript to a number of different publishers at the same time is up to you. The chances of your first novel being accepted by two publishers at the same time are remote. However, having to tell a publisher that you have already accepted a better offer can mean the end of any possible future relationship with that publisher. If you submit a photocopied manuscript, make it clear that your reason is to maintain the original. If you are submitting to more than one publisher, be up front about it. Your manuscript may not be read, however you will save possible embarrassment.

It is not necessary to include your social security number, the rights you are offering for sale (e.g. subsidiary rights, which are covered later), or a copyright notice on your manuscript. These are considered signs of an amateur. The rights for sale is something that is negotiated after the publisher expresses interest in your work.

When sending manuscripts or query letters to publishers or editors, it is considered a courtesy to include a self-addressed envelope, or address label, and sufficient postage to cover the return trip. This act should guarantee a reply. If you don't include an envelope and postage, editors customarily will not return your manuscript.

Agents

One of the questions most frequently asked by beginning writers is, "Do I need an agent?"

The answer is, "Yes and no."

First, let's consider what an agent does. A literary agent is the author's business representative. His duties include marketing manuscripts generated by the author, negotiating contracts with publishers, and following up on the various details associated with the publishing process. In addition, many agents work in the author's behalf by introducing their clients to editors, helping authors formulate ideas for books, passing along leads from editors, collecting book reviews, examining royalty statements, and generally working to promote the career of the author.

In exchange for the services provided, the author pays his agent between ten and twenty percent of his royalties, plus expenses. Agents who provide editorial services for their clients can be expected to earn a larger fee. Agents' commissions vary and are negotiated when the author signs with the agent.

For the beginning novelist, the question of whether or not to seek an agent is a difficult one to answer. There are publishers who will not read manuscripts unless they are submitted by a recognized literary agent. On the other hand, few agents will even open manuscripts from unpublished authors.

Although it may seem difficult to break this circle, there are accepted ways to approach the agent/publisher dilemma. The first thing you need is a book-length manuscript. Many agents do actively search fiction magazines for new writers. Few, however, are interested in beginning a relationship with an author who produces only short fiction.

Agents who are interested in reading material from new authors can be found in the back of writing magazines. In addition, a list of agents appears in "Literary Market Place" (LMP), which is available in the reference section of larger libraries.

If you can present credentials (samples of previously published material) to an agent, you will have a distinct advantage. Otherwise, it's best to send a query letter to a prospective agent stating your interest in being represented and including a brief synopsis of your book or play. If you sell yourself well enough in your letter and your story seems to have potential, the agent may ask for a complete outline and a sample chapter. There are hundreds of agents out there and you may have to contact a dozen or more before you find one that is interested in reading more of your material. This process, though, may take you several months and temporarily stall the progress of getting your book published.

A better alternative for a new writer is to not start looking for an agent until he has made his first sale. Once your story has been accepted for publication, you can contact an agent and be fairly certain of his interest in representing you. Don't think that you've done all the work in selling the story and that an agent won't do anything to earn his commission. At least half the work comes after the publisher agrees to purchase the manuscript. In addition, first books rarely make big money for the parties involved. Both the publisher and the agent will hope to break even on a first book. Their interest in an author lies in the potential they see in successive works.

Whether you negotiate your first sale or leave that to an agent, you will need to seek the advice of an attorney and an accountant early. Your attorney should review any contract you make with your agent or publisher and explain every item to your complete understanding. Such a contract (not all agents use contracts) may contain a termination clause which requires the author to give thirty days to a full year notification before leaving the agency. It may also stipulate that, even after the author and agent have parted company, the agent will still receive commissions from royalties the author earns from any book placed by that agent for as long as that book is sold under the terms of the original contract.

When the time comes for you to sign your first publishing contract, legal representation is no less important. Although it is rare for a publisher to take advantage of an author, it is best that you understand every facet of the contract you sign to avoid misunderstandings in the future.

Because literary agents don't act as financial managers, the author is well-advised to contact a CPA or tax attorney before he begins earning a substantial income. Accounting professionals can show the writer how to manage the rather sporadic income generated by royalties while planning for a healthy financial future.

Royalties And Advances

The most common method publishers use for compensating authors is royalties. A royalty is a percentage of the sale price of a book and is paid to the author after the sale is made. Royalty rates for hardback books begin at ten percent of the list price of the book and may graduate up to fifteen or even twenty percent, depending on the number of books sold. Royalties for mass market paperbacks are less, starting at eight percent and going up to ten percent, but rarely more.

An advance is a down-payment from the publisher based on what he thinks will be the popularity of the book. It is something like a good-faith payment, to keep the author solvent until sales begin. First novels seldom merit more than a few thousand dollars in advances. A subsequent novel from a best-selling author may command an advance of a million dollars or more. In today's environment, where a single book can earn a publisher millions, the competition in acquiring top manuscripts is fierce. Some authors actually auction their books to the highest bidder.

As an example of how royalties and advances work, imagine a publisher has expressed an interest in your novel. He has offered you a $5,000 advance against a royalty of ten percent of the book's cover price. The advance will be paid in three installments: one-third when you return the signed contract, one-third when you complete the first revision, and the final one-third when the finished manuscript is accepted by him. If the book will retail for $10, you will receive $1 for every book sold. If you are advanced $5,000, the publisher must sell five thousand copies at the retail level before you will see any more royalties.

Most publishers issue royalty statements twice a year. These detail the number of books sold, number of books returned, and the projected book sales for the next six-month period. Because retailers have the right to return books which do not sell, publishers sometimes hold royalties in reserve, so the author may not see additional royalties until the third royalty statement. These details should be clearly spelled out in the publishing contract.

In the past ten years, publishers have been willing to gamble huge sums of money to gain the right to publish books which they believe will become best-sellers. The problem with this is that few books achieve best-seller status and, therefore, don't earn their advances.

Subsidiary Rights

Publishers often negotiate with authors for rights above and beyond hardcover publication rights. These are subsidiary rights and include: paperback rights, foreign language rights, motion picture rights, theatrical performing rights, magazine reprint rights, anthology rights, and book club rights. In essence, the publisher acts as the author's agent in selling these rights and shares in their royalties. The publisher's percentage usually ranges from fifty percent for book club rights, down to fifteen percent for motion picture rights.

Some publishers actually make more money on subsidiary rights than they do on the sale of a hardcover book. For this reason, some publishers may take a chance on an unknown author if the opportunities for subsidiary sales look promising.

As the author, you have the option of retaining the subsidiary rights in part or in total, and selling them on your own. Unless you are an established author with a proven track record, it is best to let the publisher handle the subsidiary rights. He has the expertise and the contacts that will make this more profitable for both of you.

Copyright

Copyright is a form of protection provided by law for the authors of original works, including literary, dramatic, musical, artistic, and certain other intellectual works. It gives the owner of the copyright the exclusive right to reproduce the copyrighted work, to prepare derived works, to distribute copies, and to perform and display the copyrighted work publicly.

Prior to 1978, copyrights were granted for twenty-eight years and were renewable for twenty-eight more.

Since 1978, the period during which a copyright remains in effect is the author's entire life, plus fifty years. This allows that a copyrighted work that is still earning money can become a valuable part of the author's estate after his death. If the rights are sold, the value of the piece is enhanced because the rights will belong to the owner for longer than they would have under the old law.

The copyright law states that a manuscript written by you is your exclusive property under statutory law until such time as it is published. When published, a copyright notice is printed on the book and the copyright is registered with the U. S. Copyright Office in Washington, D.C. This means you, as the author, are automatically protected even as you are writing your book. It is considered the sign of a novice to include a copyright notice on the finished manuscript. In most cases, the publisher will register the copyright for the author. This will be covered in your contract. Some publishers will shy away from books that have already been copyrighted by their authors.

More complete information on copyright can be requested from the Copyright Office, Library of Congress, Washington, D.C. 20559.

Publishing Timetables

The time between when your manuscript is accepted for publication and the time the finished book hits the bookstore shelf will vary from six months to two years. Because timing is important in publishing, your book may be held longer before release or rushed to market.

During this inbetween time many separate activities take place which will all come together in the finished book. It's important to realize that the writer's work does not end with the signing of a publishing contract. You can expect to do rewrites, you'll be called on to discuss publicity and promotion, type will be set and proof sheets will be pulled for your review, several covers will be designed and, with the advice of others, one will be chosen, and your book will be integrated into the overall plans of the publisher.

It's important to remember that dozens of people will be working on your book and that any delay has a domino effect which could seriously effect your book's success. Make sure you adhere to deadlines for rewrites and proofs.

Publishing Alternatives

There are alternatives to having your book published through a regular publishing house, including: self publishing, cooperative publishing, and vanity publishing.

If you choose to self-publish your book, you will be taking on all the work of getting your manuscript typeset, printed, and distributed. This is highly risky and should only be attempted if your goal is to have total control of the finished product. The cost for publishing a single volume on your own can run as high as $12,000 for 5,000 copies. In addition to handling the manufacturing details, you'll also have to advertise and promote your book, handle all the sales, and warehouse and distribute the finished product. This could easily turn into a full-time job, taking you away from writing altogether. Unless you are looking for a career in publishing, concentrate on writing and leave the publishing headaches to someone else.

Another option is cooperative, or subsidy, publishing. Technically, this is quite different from vanity publishing, which is covered next. As the term implies, in cooperative publishing the author helps defray the publishing costs. Your up-front costs may be as little as $100, with the printer keeping and distributing half of the books printed, up to several thousand dollars to cover the total cost of production, with the printer receiving a percentage of the sales. Because they share in the risk, subsidy publishers screen manuscripts as carefully as regular publishers. In addition to your initial investment, you may still have the chore of warehousing, sales, and distribution. Alternately, the publisher may handle distribution and pay you a royalty on each book sold. There are no guarantees that you will make any profits on your book, or that you will even make back your initial investment.

Although cooperative publishing is a legitimate form of publishing, the author must be aware of what he is getting into in the beginning. Cooperative publishers are in business to make money and are, therefore, not generally interested in furthering the career of writers. If a manuscript has been rejected by regular publishers, it will often be rejected by a cooperative publisher as well.

The final alternative, vanity publishing, is not really an alternative at all. In the publishing world, vanity presses are viewed as non-legitimate. With a vanity press, the author pays the entire cost of publishing and distribution, and is often forced to pay the wholesale price for personal copies of the book. The vanity publisher makes his money not from printing and selling books, but from the egos of writers. The costs associated with a vanity publisher vary widely, but it's not unusual to be charged $10,000 for a small book.

Some vanity publishers are well-known. Others work out of small offices, changing their names and locations frequently. Horror stories exist about people turning over their life savings to have a book published, only to have the publisher disappear with their money.

There are vanity publishers that have been in business for many years, and they generally turn out a decent-looking book. However, because they accept almost any manuscript for publication, the quality of content is low, and bookstores often will not buy books published by the vanity houses. At the very least, you will personally have to go out and sell your book.

The costs involved in dealing with a vanity publisher extend beyond monetary. Editors view an author who uses a vanity press as being egotistic and gullible. Once a book has been printed by a vanity press, you can expect that no legitimate publisher will touch it. If you can't sell your manuscript to a real publisher, it is best to either re-write it or put it away in a desk drawer until the market changes.

For the writer who seeks a career in writing, it is best to concentrate on writing, rather than on publishing. Leave the publishing to the professionals. Legitimate publishers are very good at their business. They know what will sell and what won't. If your manuscript is good enough to be printed, it will be good enough for a regular publisher. If it has been rejected time and again, you need to re-evaluate your product.

Making Ends Meet

It has been said that only about fifteen percent of all writers earn their living writing. That means that for every successful writer there are six who are struggling. These odds aren't all that bad considering that it's not uncommon for there to be one hundred applicants for a single job in many fields.

The opportunities for financial rewards in writing are abundant once you establish yourself as a writer. For instance, the Writer's Guild of America, an organization which represents professional television, movie, and theatrical writers, states in their "Schedule of Minimums" that the compensation for writing a screenplay, including the treatment, can be as high as $54,888. A sixty-minute teleplay with story can earn the writer nearly $20,000. It's not unusual for a novelist to receive a $10,000 advance. Some successful novelists garner advances of a million dollars or more. The possiblities are staggering.

For the beginning author, however, the financial rewards are often smaller and intermittent. The possibility of big money is enough to keep many would-be novelists typing. Others find that any monetary reward can provide a real ego boost.

While you're working on your novel or screenplay, consider free-lance writing as a way of keeping your skills sharp and your pockets lined. Pay varies with the job and your experience, but you can expect up to $25 per hour.

Free-lance writers provide writing and editing services for any number of businesses, magazines, and organizations. Freelancers produce newsletters, fiction and non-fiction for magazines, press releases, advertising jingles, corporate reports, slide presentations, and more. This is where business cards and contacts come in handy. Networking (going out and meeting people who can put you in touch with potential customers) is important. Let your friends and relatives know that you're in business for yourself.

Writing contests offer writers an opportunity for monetary rewards and recognition. You can find contests listed in most writing journals.

Other possibilities include teaching writing classes, lecturing, and ghostwriting.

If you are going to sell yourself as a writer, it's important that you develop your own promotional material. This is like a resume with selling copy. Your "brochure" doesn't need to be more than a page, but it must offer a real incentive for the reader to hire you instead of doing the writing himself.

Professional Organizations

There are two types of professional organizations in which writers involve themselves: those organizations which cater to the writer's ego, and those which serve his career.

Typically, the first type of organization is local in nature and is a place where want-to-be writers meet and socialize. You say something nice about a writer's unpublished work, and he says something nice about yours. Sometimes there are speakers or a writer will give a reading, but more often than not, all this type of organization does is take the writer away from what he should be doing: writing.

The second type of organization offers something the writer can use, such as services and information. This might include legal services, market news, advice on ethics and contracts, literary criticism, educational opportunities, grants and awards, and insurance plans. Membership fees in these organizations vary from $10 to $150 annually. They include, among others, the American Society of Journalists and Authors, The Author's Guild, the National Writer's Club, the Poetry Society of America, and the Society of Children's Book Writers. You can often find these organizations listed in the same books and magazines which list writing markets.

Professional Ethics

It has been said that publishing is one of the few honorable professions left in the world. As in any activity where money changes hands, there are opportunities for dishonesty.

Generally, publishers will not cheat their authors because without authors a publisher will have nothing to publish. In addition, you have the right to expect that a publisher, as well as those working directly for him, will be honest with you, will abide by the terms of any contracts signed by him, will respond to you in a timely manner, will not plagiarize your work, and will treat you fairly.

In exchange for his professional behavior, a publisher expects you to be honest with him, to provide original and accurate work, to represent yourself honestly, never to promise something you can't deliver, and to abide by the terms of any contract you sign.

These are the legal areas of professionalism. There are two additional areas which fall under the heading of temperament. Editors and publishers loathe writers who are constant whiners. An editor is not intended to be the writer's therapist or secretary. He is a business partner. He cares about the writer's personal life only in so far as it affects his work. Some writers develop close relationships with their editors. This is only natural. But don't expect your editor to ignore his twenty other writers and assorted other duties to be at your beck and call.

Another area that causes editors grief is deadlines. For some reason, many authors don't realize the importance of sticking to deadlines. In publishing, timing is everything. There will be dozens of people involved in a single publishing project, from editors and proofreaders to typesetters and printers. If one person misses a deadline, the entire schedule can fall behind.

Consider this example: Working two months in advance, the printer has scheduled press time for your book for the first week in March. As the writer, you were to give the final approval on the proofs before they went to the platemaker. Because you held onto the proofs until the last week of February, the printer couldn't get the printing plates made in time and had to bump your project to the next available time, two months away. That caused the bindery to bump you to their next available time, three months away. With time for reviewing and promotion, the publication date of your book could end up in October. Worse yet, the publisher may decide that Autumn is a bad time to release a book like your's and may hold it over until the next Spring. This may sound unbelievable, but it happens. Books deals have actually been lost because of production delays caused by authors. The bottom line is: don't make promises you can't keep, and keep every promise that you make.

Writing Exercises

Compose a query letter to an editor asking for permission to submit a book-length manuscript. Use the LMP to select a publishing company and an editor in that company. Be sure to include any previous writing credentials (skip this if you are unpublished - never fabricate credentials), what qualifies you to tell this story, and a short, interest-grabbing summary of the story. Remember, provide just enough information to get the editor interested in reading more, don't reveal how the story ends.

You may want to expand you writing skills by free-lancing your services. Now is a good time to begin work on a brochure which advertises your abilities. Prepare a one-page flyer. You can find samples of writers' advertisements in writing magazines and other types of advertising in your library. In this piece you are selling yourself as a writer, so the wording is important.

10

Markets for Fiction

With completed manuscript in hand, you are now ready to send your book off to a publisher or your screenplay to a producer. The question is, of the thousands of places to sell fiction in the United States, where will you start?

Actually, this is a question you should have asked before you started writing. It's important to know if a market exists for a particular type of story before you spend six months to a year developing it. Since most writers are unwilling to let the market dictate their story direction, you won't be alone if thoughts of selling your work come as an afterthought.

Finding a buyer is the most important part of writing. If your story never gets published or produced, your ideas will never be disseminated, which is the reason for writing in the first place.

Instead of listing the names and addresses of potential buyers for your manuscript, this chapter is intended to review the different categories of markets for fiction and provide some direction as to where best to look for a sale.

Market References

The standard reference book for writer's in all fictional genre is "Writer's Market," published annually by Writer's Digest Books. This book contains one of the most comprehensive listings of markets in a format specifically designed to help writers choose a publisher. In addition to 4,000 names, "Writer's Market" also includes addresses, names of editors to contact, submission requirements, manuscript lengths and form, payments rates, business policies, and helpful information provided by editors. Because this book is updated annually, you can invest in a new copy every year or you can rely on finding the most recent edition at your library. Key information in the publishing world changes rapidly, so make sure you are using the most current edition.

Another good source for tracking down book publishers is the "LMP: Literary Market Place, the directory of American book publishing." This large volume lists publishers of every size, along with the names of the key personnel. It also lists editorial services and agents, professional associations, courses, and awards.

Small publishers, the advantages of which will be discussed later, are yet another potential market for books. The "International Directory of Little Magazines & Small Presses," published by Dustbooks, contains information about small presses and the types of manuscripts they are interested in reading. You should be able to find this book in a metropolitan or large university library.

Assorted markets can be found in writing magazines like "Writer's Digest" and "The Writer." Publishers of books and magazine editors use these writing magazines to solicit manuscripts and story ideas. Because these magazines are issued monthly, the information contained in them is timely.

If film is your area of interest, you should become familiar with the trade publications for the industry: "Variety," "The Hollywood Reporter," and "Broadcasting." These will keep you up to date on what type of stories are being produced, along with the names of people who are doing the producing.

Finally, keep your ears open. There may be market opportunities right in your own neighborhood. Universities, as well as civic groups, often publish anthologies of short fiction using the work of local authors. With recent changes in the laws affecting cable television, cable companies are required to develop public access policies, putting program production capabilities in the hands of anyone with a script. And, local theatrical groups are always looking for original plays to perform.

Demographics

No marketing plan can exist without reference to demographics. Demographics is the study of statistical populations with respect to their age, gender, income, size, and distribution. It is a topic which is as important to the fiction writer as to any advertising executive on Madison Avenue.

To the publisher, demographics is of prime importance. The marketer is interested, above all, in who is going to buy a particular book, pay admission to view a movie, or sit through commercials in order to see a television program.

Before buying a manuscript, the publisher or producer is going to determine to whom the piece will appeal. He has to choose men, women, children, or adolescents. Next he will break the audience down by specific age, socio-economic level, and even geographic location.

Whether knowing it or not, this is the same process the writer used early in the creation of the work in question. At the point of conception, the writer had an idea of for whom the story was being written. The author didn't begin writing a children's story, only to have it turn into a two-hundred page horror novel. Likewise, a romance novel, targeted toward women between the ages of 21 and 35, would not turn into a western. The audience is selected and the story, from beginning to end, must keep that audience in mind.

For some reason, upon the completion of the manuscript, many writers forget who their audience is. They have spent up to a year focusing on a single segment of humanity, only to acquire blurred vision at the end. It's not uncommon for an author to send a science fiction manuscript to a publisher of westerns. By the same token, spicy adult romances, from time to time, make their way to religious publishers. This is a costly error, not only for the writer, but also for the recipient of the manuscript. It's important to remember who your audience is before, during, and after the writing.

Knowing the specific audience you intend to reach makes the job of selling your story a little easier. The ''Writer's Market'' tells you what type of books a publisher publishes and what type of stories magazines will print. All you have to do is match the story you have written to a publisher. This is as easy as it sounds. What's more, most directories categorize markets to take the work out of location.

Book Markets

Of the more than 40,000 books which are published every year, approximately 6,000 are fiction. You can visit any bookstore and judge which genre supports the most titles.

In book publishing, some companies produce only a single genre (e.g. Harlequin Books), while others are more broad-based (e.g. Harper & Row Publishers). While there are more than 800 book publishers listed in the ''Writer's Market,'' you should not be disheartened. Just start at the beginning and eliminate as you go. Mark the publishers that print the type of book you have written, and skip the rest. In a short time, you should have a list of ten or twenty possibles. Pare that down to one or two, compose a letter, and get the ball rolling. You don't need to go all the way through the list before you send out your first query. While your manuscript is out, you'll have plenty of time to come up with more potential buyers.

There are several things to consider when you are looking for a publisher. First, big is not necessarily best. In fact, the bigger publishing houses frequently won't accept manuscripts from unpublished or unagented authors. Don't try to fight this as you will only waste your time. Instead, look to the smaller publishers, those who only release six to ten titles a year. Frequently these are overlooked, but are often receptive to giving new authors a chance.

Another important consideration is the number of submissions a publisher receives in a year. If a publisher receives 5,000 submissions annually, you know the competition will be tough. If, on the other hand, you are only competing with 49 other manuscripts, you can expect your story will get a little more personal attention. By now you should expect that you aren't going to get rich off of your first novel. Just getting your book published is an admirable goal. Once your first book is in print, subsequent books will be easier to sell and will bring in more money. With that in mind, look for publishers who offer small advances, or no advance at all. These companies may be willing to take more of a chance on an unpublished author.

As stated before, if your manuscript does not match the profile offered by the publisher, don't waste your time by thinking your book will make them change. Editors take from two to four weeks to respond to a query, and four to twelve weeks for a completed manuscript. Since it actually takes only a day or two to evaluate a manuscript, your novel will spend up to three months sitting. That translates into four or five submissions in a year, so each one must truly be on target.

Magazine Markets

Every writer of a book-length manuscript automatically expects that his story will be published as a book. Unfortunately, many authors overlook the possibility of serializing their stories in a magazine.

"Writer's Digest" lists more than 1,400 consumer magazines. Fortunately for authors, the categories are clearly delineated so you need not search through all of the listings individually. On the other hand, there is no all-encompassing category for "fiction."

Magazine fiction follows the same genre we have seen before, with a few variations. Whereas our fictional genre were divided into romance and westerns, magazines are targeted to more specific demographics; specifically, women and men. Knowing who the story was written for makes this transition quite easy. A women's magazine is a potential buyer of romance fiction, while a men's magazine may buy a western. Mystery, science fiction, fantasy, and horror are still covered by their own magazines. In addition, there are regional and literary magazines which buy short fiction, condensed novels, or serials.

In seeking to publish your story in a magazine, you may have to modify your manuscript. Few periodicals can afford to allow the space needed for a 100,000 word story, even over two or three issues. Here is where your editing ability comes in. You should be able to take your novel and compress it into 6,000 words, while still keeping the character development and plot, or you might choose to excerpt a couple of chapters. ''Reader's Digest'' has been doing this successfully for years.

One of the benefits of publishing fiction in magazines is that you can sell the same story more than one time. The first magazine that buys your story buys the first serial rights. Some magazines will only buy first rights, but others will buy second serial rights. When you offer a previously-published story to a magazine you need to make it clear that you are offering second serial rights.

Script Markets

As mentioned earlier, breaking into film and television is difficult. Opportunities are infrequent unless you have unusual talent or help with introductions. That's not to say that these markets are completely closed. With simplified production techniques, small studios are slowly moving in to compete with major production facilities, and these new companies want to attract new writers.

Approaching television markets offers the fewest alternatives. Scripts are written for individual television shows, which are produced by one of several production companies. In the case of television scripts, it's important that you begin corresponding with the production company early in the creative process. The needs of production companies literally change on a daily basis. A show you watched last night may already have been cancelled for the next season. Getting your foot in the door is often the most difficult part. In addition to reading the trade magazines and looking through ''Writer's Market,'' a good way to get started as a television writer is by taking a college course in television production or taking a job as a writer at a local television station.

The opportunities in film are often less glamorous for beginning writers, but they do exist. Flexibility is the key. Don't set out to write a major motion picture, only to have it rejected by the major studios. Start with a documentary or a children's movie. A documentary requires the same basic skills as a commercial film. Once you have a documentary or two in your resume, producers will be more receptive to your proposals and agents will answer your phone calls.

A similar stategy works for theater. It is naive to think you can start at the top in any type of business. Writing is no different. After you have written a theatrical script, try selling it locally. You may end up giving it away to a community theater, along with your time to direct the play. If you have written a good play and you demonstrate ability in its execution, you won't have to work as hard for subsequent sales.

In writing, as in other businesses, talent and hard work are rewarded. But the writer must not approach the market with a chip on his shoulder. Until you have something published, you are a novice. No matter how well your words flow, you won't be recognized as a writer until you've made a sale or two. Accept this, and don't expect to win a Pulitzer Prize in your first year. Keep writing in your journal, keep practicing the elements of fiction, and you will progress.

Writing Exercises

Now that you have seen the fiction writing business from beginning to end, it is time for you to formulate a business plan. This plan should extend for a period of three years and should set reachable goals for each six-month period. Reachable goals are important, since unattained goals will eat away at your self image. In addition to writing down the goals, also include how these goals will be realized. Give this business plan some thought and post it on the wall where you can see it. Update it as necessary. Most important, don't give up. The work ahead is hard, but if you keep at it you can succeed.

Supplemental Writing Exercises

These supplemental writing exercises are meant to stimulate your thought process during those times in your writing career when words and ideas flow with difficulty. They should be used independently of any of the preceding chapters and are especially useful for developing journal entries. Though these exercises don't relate directly to any individual chapter, you should focus on applying what you have learned throughout this text.

1. Writing must be as visual a form of communication as painting. A painter knows that it takes literally hundreds of individual colors to create a portrait. Something as seemingly simple as a cloud isn't made up of a single color of gray, but is a blending of dozens of shades of gray, white, and black.

As a writer, you must be able to communicate the same information in words that a painter communicates in colors. Visual communication skills are something you must constantly work at sharpening.

As an exercise in visual thinking, obtain a paint chip sample card (six to ten shades of a single color) from a hardware store or paint dealer.

In your journal, give each color a name (e.g., Prussian Blue) and then write a paragraph describing the color. Be creative in your description, but make certain that someone who has never seen this color will know exactly what you are talking about. You should include examples of where you might find this color (e.g., the deep blue of the sky on a clear morning, just before sunrise). The more details you include, the better.

2. Take an outing to a public place such as a park, a shopping center, or an airport. Sit for some time with your eyes closed. Concentrate on exercising those senses which usually take a back seat to your vision. Listen to the sounds around you. Feel the temperature and movement of the air. Notice how it changes when someone walks by. Think about the smells which abound.

When you return to your journal, write two pages which describe your experience without using any visual descriptions. To make it more interesting, you may want to use some elements of plotting to explain why you could not see.

3. You are the last living creature on earth. In a short story, tell how you came to have this distinction and how you will go about your life. As a twist, consider that you encounter a plant that has the ability to communicate. How would this change your life? How might it threaten your existence?

4. Write a scene of dialogue where two strangers are riding on a bus and one of them begins talking to the other. One character is very talkative, wanting to share some details of his personal life. The other character isn't interested in talking, but will listen, just the same.

The goal here is to introduce the two characters through the use of their dialogue and their actions. By the end, your reader should feel as if he knows these people and could recognize them if he saw them on the street.

5. The scene: There are five people in a wooden life boat in the middle of the ocean. Their luxury liner has just burned and sunk. The life boat is old and in poor repair. The passengers realize that this small craft will sink before they can possibly be rescued.

The problem: There are only four life jackets.

Using dialogue, write an account of these five people as they decide who among them will go down with the life boat.

6. Write a two-page essay which compares and contrasts two disimilar characters. Keep in mind some of the options which were discussed in Chapter 4. Even though this is a short exercise, make certain that you organize your narration so your reader will know about which character you are talking. Practice using general-to-specific description.

7. Pick up a women's magazine and flip through it looking at make-up advertisements (these are the ones with the close-ups of the models). Tear out one of the ads and take it to your writing area.

In your journal, write several pages which decribe the woman in the picture. Use a Character Map as a checklist to make sure you include enough details.

When you begin outlining a story, this is a good technique for casting characters. A photograph of a real person can help you describe that character more clearly.

8. Set aside a section of your journal and label it "Characters." Whenever you meet, hear about, or read about an interesting character, use this section to write a short profile about that character. The purpose of this exercise is to give you a group of characters you can draw upon when you are "casting" a story. In fact, one of these profiles might become the central figure of an entire story.

Since you can't use real people as characters in your stories, don't be afraid to embellish the truth. In other words, develop the character to make him or her even more interesting. Make up missing details. Exaggerate mannerisms.

9. Fictionalizing events is an important skill for a writer. A fictionalized event is one which could have happened, but probably not as it is told; ordinary events which are made extraordinary through the writer's skill and imagination.

Select a short newspaper article (remember, reading is one of your best sources of inspiration) and rewrite it in a fictionalized form. Your version should take a story which has minimal news value and present it as one you would see on the front page.

10. The following exercise is intended to help you realize the power and flexibility of words.

Imagine that a space traveler has landed on our planet. He does not speak your language and you cannot communicate in his language. However, he does have a translation dictionary for English. He opens the dictionary and points to a word that means "bread".

Your job is to write a description of bread as you would describe it to someone who knows nothing about it. The trick is, because the visitor will have to look up every word, you must limit your description to ten words.

You should focus on describing how bread smells, its taste, how it feels, and what it looks like. The longer you spend thinking about this assignment, the more benefit you will gain.

light brown
For eating - oblong - made with wheat & yeast - can be spongey feel sliced + buttered

Epilogue

You have now reached the end of this small part of your training as a professional writer. The next step is up to you. You, and you alone, control your destiny. You are the only one who can shape your future.

As stated on page one of this book, no one can teach you how to become a writer of fiction. No book ever written has turned anyone into a fiction writer. That's just not how it happens. However, through the diligent application of the techniques contained in this book, along with a high degree of personal drive and ambition, you can turn yourself into a writer.

Having read this book and completed the writing exercises, you have gained the basic knowledge needed to become a fiction writer. Now you must begin to put your newly-acquired knowledge to work.

If, after all this, you still have the desire to write, you are halfway toward realizing your goal. Think of yourself as your own personal trainer. Be a tough coach. Above all, don't quit. There will be hard times at first, but you must take setbacks in stride and continue moving forward.

No matter how good a writer you become, you must continue to practice your craft every day and to polish your skills continuously. Seize every opportunity to use the tools of your newly chosen trade. Delight in discovering new words. Revel in their eloquent use.

For now, the important thing is to start writing, keep writing, and don't give up.

Twelve Precepts of Fiction Writing

1. You must want to write.
2. Writing is a business. Treat it accordingly.
3. Read what others write.
4. Keep a daily journal.
5. Know your audience.
6. Write from experience.
7. Don't tell, show.
8. Get to the point.
9. Follow accepted grammar, spelling, and punctuation.
10. Be your own harshest critic.
11. Rewrite, rewrite, rewrite.
12. Be patient and don't lose your vision.

Index

Flower Duet
music by
Delibe (?)